Won't You Love Me?

Also by Toni Maguire

Won't You Love Me?

Unloved as a girl, abused as a woman – the true
story of Ava's fight for survival

TONI MAGUIRE

with Ava Thomas

First published in the UK by John Blake Publishing
An imprint of Bonnier Books UK
4th Floor, Victoria House
Bloomsbury Square
London WC1B 4DA
England

Owned by Bonnier Books
Sveavägen 56, Stockholm, Sweden

www.facebook.com/johnblakebooks
twitter.com/jblakebooks

Paperback – 978-1-789-465-21-1
eBook – 978-1-789-465-22-8
Audiobook – 978-1-789-466-19-5

A CIP catalogue of this book is available from the British Library.

Design by www.envydesign.co.uk
Printed and bound in Great Britain by Clays Ltd, Elcograf S.p.A.

1 3 5 7 9 10 8 6 4 2

For each paperback book sold, Bonnier Books UK shall donate 2.5% of its net receipts to the NSPCC (registered charity numbers 216401 and SC037717).

The authors of this work want to show Ava Thomas' experience growing up and so you will find language in this book which may be offensive. It is used to show the reality of the author's experience and they and the Publisher would like to add a trigger warning for that here.

This book is a work of non-fiction, based on the life, experiences and recollections of Ava Thomas. Certain details in this story, including names and locations, have been changed to protect the identity and privacy of the authors, their family and those mentioned.

John Blake Publishing is an imprint of Bonnier Books UK
www.bonnierbooks.co.uk

*To my son and daughter. Without you both,
I would not be the woman I am today. You make
me proud every day, I can't wait to see how your
wonderful lives unfold.*

Contents

Author's Note
from Toni Maguire

When Ava first contacted me, I immediately found her story of interest; mainly because it was different from all the others I have written. In nearly all of my previous books, I needed to begin with the person's early years.

Ava's story, on the other hand, seemed different. I wrote back asking for a little more information which she sent me by return and as soon as I read it, I decided that this book is one I needed to write, and also would need to start with her adult experiences. Why alter the formula? Well, because there were so many decisions made in Ava's teens and twenties that showed me how her unhappy childhood had shaped her. Those in charge of her tried their best to brainwash her into adopting their prejudices, and eventually she rebelled against it. She really fought to become the person she wanted to be, drawing on her inner courage and determination.

I arranged for the both of us to meet and she arrived with

her daughter Jade. Apart from being a very pretty and friendly child, Jade exuded self-confidence. This self-assurance was exactly what Ava had wished for Jade's childhood. She also talked to me about her son Justin, who was turning thirteen. He was staying with friends so couldn't meet me too, but Ava told me that despite his early trauma, he was already a pretty confident and independent child, working hard at school and with a wide circle of friends. Ava's dream for her children was for them to choose good careers and become financially and emotionally independent. When the time came for them to enter relationships, she wanted them to make their choices wisely, unlike her experiences when she was in her teens.

Over the months of writing her story, we have had extensive calls and countless messages as she told me her story and answered my questions. Over that time, I felt I really got to know Ava. I admired her determination and her attitudes. She said repeatedly to me that she did not want to be seen as a victim but as a woman who, having put the past firmly behind her, was in charge of her life; a life she had worked so hard to make successful.

I am so happy that she has overcome so much and found so much happiness for herself and her children.

Toni Maguire, June 2022

Prologue

The picture behind my eyes, the one that will not leave me, is of a woman with a tiny baby tucked into a pink, blood-splattered carrier strapped to her heaving chest. She's standing in the middle of the road, her eyes wide with fright as she screams for help. Doors open, neighbours rush out and she pleads with them to call the police. 'Call them now!' she shrieks when, as though in shock, not one of them has made a move to summon help. Their horrified eyes are focused not on the woman's bruised and bleeding face, but on the blood splatters on the baby's carrier and clothes.

'He's going to kill me this time, please someone help me, DO something,' she wails.

A hand falls on her shoulder and, looking up, she sees the head of their local GP. 'I've already called them,' he says both to her and to the neighbours standing transfixed, watching the scene play out. 'Come with me, Ava, my surgery isn't open yet so there's only my wife inside. Your face is bleeding and I want to have a quick look at your baby.'

'It's my blood on her, Dr Khan, but my son, he's still in there. Dave grabbed hold of him when I tried to get him to come with me,' she gasps.

'The police will get him out for you,' the doctor tells her as he takes her arm gently and walks her through the gaping throng. The woman can hear the murmurs of sympathetic comments coming from her neighbours, which tells her that they have no hesitation in believing her story for they have heard the screams of pain and the aggressive shouting both in the daytime and at all hours of the night. And they have seen her bruised face and split lips when, with no pride left inside her, she limped painfully to the shops to buy food for her family's meals.

Click! The next picture comes into place.

The woman, hearing the approaching sirens, is gazing out of the doctor's waiting-room window when she sees two police cars pull up outside the house which had once been her home. She can hear the sounds of them banging on the door, which remains firmly closed – though not for long as the police shout through the letter box that if the man doesn't open it straight away, they will break it down.

'Why two cars?' she asks the doctor's wife, who is standing beside her.

'Because you will have to go to the station as well. They will need a statement from you before they charge him,' she explains. 'My husband has already emailed them a report of the dates and nature of all your previous injuries. He wants to make sure that this time Dave is arrested and charged.'

'And, Ava,' the doctor adds, 'whatever you do, don't go

back to him. Not this time; if not for your sake, then for your children's. Your baby was already in that carrier, wasn't she, when he attacked you?'

The woman just nods her head as she watches the man who has been her partner for over six years being dragged, protesting loudly and abusively, out of the house. The man she once loved so much. The man who was the father of her two children.

The man she knew she had to leave.

As if reading her thoughts, for a moment he raises his head and looks straight across the street to where she is. She knows if she was closer, she would see in those large brown eyes of his the unbridled hatred lurking there.

At the same time as the policeman places his hand on the man's head to tell him that he must climb into the back of the car, to her relief she sees the policewoman emerge from the house, holding the hand of a small, sobbing boy. She bends down to say something, which makes the little boy tug at her hand. It's clear he wants to walk as fast as he can to where his mother is for he too has seen her at the window. The woman opens the surgery door, hugs him tightly and murmurs soothing words of comfort before wiping his tears away tenderly.

The policewoman asks the doctor if the woman is able to go to the station to make a statement. 'Yes,' he answers and gently secures the baby back in her carrier, still resting on the woman's chest.

'Remember what I told you,' the doctor says quietly as he opens the door to let them leave.

'Yes,' she murmurs.

She climbs into the car, where the driver has been waiting patiently. After securing the boy and the woman's seat belts in the back, the policewoman takes the passenger seat in front.

As they drive off, the woman's blank face presses against the window. She sees the door to the house which has been her home for the last six years. A door she has to accept that she will never walk through again.

The policewoman turns around slightly to look at her: 'Is there someone we can call?'

'There's no one,' says the woman who once was me.

1

When we pulled up outside the police station, my body was just so stiff that the policewoman, without making a comment, gave me her hand and gently helped me out. My baby, thank goodness, was still sleeping; totally unaware of what had been happening all around her. Oh, Jade had cried out when he attacked me, but more from indignation at being woken up than anything else. On the other hand, my four-year-old son, Justin, was old enough to understand that his dad beating me was wrong. He had not uttered a word since he was brought over to me. I could tell instinctively that he was still frightened and in shock. The police shouting through the door would also have scared him and he must have been wondering just what was going to happen next.

Goodness knows what his father had said to him before he was dragged out. From the moment Justin was old enough to be placed in his playpen, he had seen and heard far too much. Already he was having nightmares and calling out for me in the night from his urine-soaked bedding. As we walked into the station his little hand clasped mine even tighter and he pressed himself into my body. Although he did not say a word, I could feel he wanted some answers as to where we were being taken.

I remembered that his dad had always referred to the men in blue as 'pigs' or 'scum'. Little wonder he was worried and afraid. 'We're going to meet some nice kind people,' I told him, for so far I had only seen sympathy and concern on the faces of the two constables who had brought us to the station.

The policewoman led the three of us into a room. Not one of those really stark interview rooms with only a desk and a few wooden chairs, but this one contained at least one comfortable chair and a coffee table with a box of tissues on it. Another officer, dressed in casual clothes, came into the room. She introduced herself as DI Mary Langham, 'Though you can call me Mary,' she added, giving me a friendly smile. She then told Justin that there was a special playroom nearby with lots of toys in it. 'Now I have a friend here who will show it to you and let you play there for a little while. And there's a tin of chocolate biscuits in there too. How does that sound?'

As no answer was given, I spoke for him: 'You like chocolate biscuits and ice cream too, don't you, Justin?'

'We'll get you some,' she told him before winking at me.

I don't know who was sent out on the mission to indulge my son, but someone was, I gathered from the green and brown drip stains on Justin's top when I saw him later.

'Thank you,' was all I managed to say as my son, with his mind hopefully focused on toys, biscuits and ice cream, was led away. Clearly the police had been thoughtful enough to arrange that Justin didn't have to hear everything about how his father had abused me.

*　*　*

'From what I've heard from my colleagues and read in your doctor's report, you are here because you need help and you wish to lay an assault charge. Is that right?' Mary Langham asked me.

'Yes.'

'Well, let's get some tea brought in and would you like some sandwiches as well?'

I said yes to the tea but no to food – I didn't think I could swallow a single crumb without throwing up.

'Ava, there's nothing to be worried about in here. We will make sure you get all the help you need so let's just go through a few things, OK?'

'All right.'

'There is help available, you know, and it's my job to see you get it, so don't be frightened now.'

She then asked if my baby needed feeding and I told her I had managed to do that at the doctor's surgery, so hopefully she would sleep for a while.

Her next words were to ask me to tell her about that night when my daughter was born.

*　*　*

It was feeling the rise and fall of my daughter Jade's chest as she breathed against mine that brought back every detail of the night, nearly a month earlier, when I was lucky not to have lost her. I was just so big, but from the way my tiny baby was kicking, she was telling me my womb was not large enough and that she wanted more room. Much as I already loved her, she managed to make me feel exhausted nearly all the time. I was lying on the bed, stroking my bulge, as I tried to let her know I could hardly wait for us to meet. Then Dave returned home. He must have told me to get up and make him his dinner, and maybe because I was half asleep, I snapped at him, saying that I needed to rest because the baby was due soon.

'I think that was it, but I don't really remember the exact words that were used,' I told Mary.

'So what happened next?'

'He pulled me off the bed by my hair. It was that white-hot pain that really woke me. I can see him now, staring down angrily at me. My hair was coiled round his fist and when he yanked it again, I fell heavily off the bed. I begged him to stop, I was so scared and I was crying with fear for the baby. I could hardly see straight because my tears were blinding me but I could smell his hot breath and I knew he had been drinking, which meant any excuse, even a tiny one, could send him into a rage.

'Not releasing my hair, he pulled me up so I was standing on tiptoes, begging him to think of our unborn baby. It was then that my waters broke, which sent him into even more of a fury. He shook me, called me a filthy, disgusting slut. And then his other hand turned into a fist that went straight into my face. I still tried to tell him that the baby was coming, but nothing was going to stop him. He hit me again, I saw stars, there was a blinding pain in my head and I realised he was still holding me up by my hair.

'"Don't you pretend to be knocked out, I've not finished with you yet," he warned as punch after punch landed on my ribs.

'The last one, or maybe there were more, landed on the mound of my stomach.

'I screamed at him then, saying it wasn't me but our baby that he was attacking. And you know what he said?'

'No, Ava, tell me,' Mary urged.

'That he wanted another boy, not a girl, and I hadn't even got that right. Another punch came my way before he let go of my hair, threw me onto the floor and stormed out of the house. My poor little son was screaming for me. I hated myself for leaving him behind, but all I knew was that I had to get out of the house so I crawled on my hands and knees and I got to the hall.

'My waters had broken, I couldn't give birth on that cold, hard floor. Feeling the dampness of my trousers, I knew that I hadn't the strength to change them, only enough to stagger to the door, where I stood for a moment leaning against the wall, trying to get my weak, woolly limbs to take me across the road to Dr Khan's surgery. I still don't know how I managed, I think one of my neighbours saw me and rushed over to help. I know that I collapsed the moment the doctor opened the door.'

'What's your next memory?'

'Being on a stretcher, feeling a hand patting my cheek and hearing a voice telling me I was going to be all right, that they were taking me to the hospital.

'"My son ..." I managed to gasp.

'"He's being looked after," were the last words I heard.

'It was the doctor's wife who had gone and fetched my son and calmed him down a little. She left a note for Dave, saying where we both were.'

'And then what happened?'

'You know, don't you? You've seen the doctor's notes.'

'Yes, your body was far too weak for you to have a natural birth. They had to get your baby out by a C-section.'

'It's funny, isn't it, that I came round so quickly? It was as though something inside my head was telling me to wake up and meet my daughter. The nurse placed my dark-haired, perfect little girl in my arms as she watched with a smile. And this time it was tears of joy that ran down my face. I suppose it's a good thing that a newborn's eyes can't see much of the world because when I was finally able to have a bath and looked in the mirror, I saw a face that would have frightened any child, no matter how young. Even I cringed with shock when I saw it: two eyes surrounded by dark bronze bruises spread from the bridge of my nose to the blackened circles below my eyelids. If that wasn't bad enough, there were more bruises fading from purple to yellow right across both my cheekbones.'

'Yes, I've read the report – you needed stitches near your left eye. There were bruises all over your body and you had mild concussion. Do you want me to go on?'

'No.'

'So, Ava, after that, why did you go back?'

'I had nowhere else to go and I couldn't leave my son there, could I?'

'Yes, it was your little boy who told Mrs Khan that his daddy had hurt Mummy and the baby growing inside her. And what did you tell the doctors? That you had fallen. Why?'

'I was scared social services would take my children away. At least that's what Dave told me would happen when he promised to turn over a new leaf.'

'No, that wouldn't have happened if you had agreed to leave him. A place would have been found for you straight away. But if you had said you wanted to stay, no doubt social services would have had to take them. He had already shown he was quite capable of trying to harm your daughter even before she came into the world. So, did he promise not to hit you again?'

And another picture came into my head. Him appearing at the hospital, carrying flowers and that smile of his that once made my insides melt.

'Looking up at him, I told myself he seemed so ashamed. He took my hand, told me how sorry he was and that he would make it up to me and that it would never happen again.'

'So you came home. When was that? And what crime did you commit this time that made him treat you like a punch bag?'

The detective's words might have sounded harsh, but I could tell who her anger was directed at and it wasn't me. Still, I could hardly bring myself to say anything.

'Come on, Ava, just tell me,' she persisted. 'You've not

got anything to worry about now. We'll be keeping him in overnight so we'll need to get everything sorted out long before that. But I still need to finish my report or rather, get the full details for your statement.

'Before we go through that though, please just tell me what you plan to do.'

'I don't know,' I murmured and as the reality hit me, my tears began again.

A tissue was pressed into my hand. More tea was sent for, before an arm went around my shaking shoulders.

'What I need to know is, have you made up your mind to leave him this time?'

And I heard those words of Dr Khan's – 'for the sake of your children' – rocketing around in my head.

'Yes,' I answered, though I had no idea just how I was going to escape him. 'I must put my children first. He might not ever hit my son, but he has no intention of bonding with my daughter.'

'Why?'

'She takes after me a little and she's too white, he says. So, I really have to make them safe.'

'And maybe yourself as well, Ava.'

* * *

When a knock came on the door about ten minutes later, in came two young constables, who seemed laden down with various objects. Not only was more tea and biscuits brought in but a pack of disposable nappies, baby wipes, a thick towel as well as emergency toiletry packs, all of which were placed in front of me.

'Thought you might need these,' Mary said. 'I'm sure Jade is going to need changing pretty soon.'

She was right, of course: that niggling worry of how I would manage had been there in the back of my mind for a while and already there was a strong indication in the air that a change was overdue. Once I had gone to the toilet and fixed that problem, Mary asked what had made Dave attack me so soon after I had come home from the hospital.

'You want to know about what happened this evening, don't you?'

'Yes, but only if you feel up to telling me now. There's enough information from the assault when the baby was due to charge him. We have also arranged for a place of safety for you and the children to stay in.'

Mary went on to tell me about the refuge where she had found us a safe place. No one must know its whereabouts, she emphasised. Yes, I would be allowed to go out, but if I contacted anyone, no hint of where the refuge was located must be given: 'There are some women there whose lives are in real danger,' she told me. 'There are alarms everywhere in the house and cameras positioned out of sight. There is always someone on duty and if the camera captures anyone suspicious trying to enter, one press on the alarm button brings the police racing over so I've called it a safe place because that's exactly what it is. It's a place where women are taken so that the men they have left cannot find them and cause even more trouble. So, it's up to you, Ava. Do you want to tell me now what little thing he used as an excuse to lay into you this time? But we can also do it later, if you've had enough for now. I know that sometimes it helps to get it all out in one go and hopefully it will help you to see just what is very likely to happen again if you change your mind and go back to him.'

'Thank you, I'll talk about it now,' I said, for I knew getting everything off my chest would help me. After all, Mary Langham was the first person I had met in a long time who I felt I could confide in. Over the years I had dropped my friends, not wanting them to see the bruises on my face and neck, until finally I felt I had no one left who I could talk to.

'I embarrassed him in front of his friends,' I told her.

As those words escaped my lips, pictures of the day shot into my head, making my hands shake so badly that I had to use both of them to guide my third mug of tea back down on the table.

Noticing my tremors, Mary reached over and placed a hand on mine: 'Take a deep breath, Ava, there's no rush, just take your time. I understand you've been through a really bad period.'

I gulped a little – I was still so shaken – but knowing I had to get what happened out, after a long pause, I began hesitantly: 'I was sitting in the bedroom breastfeeding Jade when he came up to me, looking his normal self, or I suppose there was just no obvious sign of temper then.

'"You're still not feeling like going out anywhere, are you?" was the first thing he said. It sounded more like an accusation than a question, though.

'"Not so soon after having Jade," was the answer I gave

him and even though the prickles on the back of my neck were telling me that he had something planned, I made myself turn on the widest smile I could.

'"Well, now, if you've decided that you and Jade shouldn't go out, then it would be good if I brought some company here, wouldn't it? Thinking of you, darlin', don't want you being on your own too much," he told me.

'The last thing I wanted was company. With feeding Jade every few hours all I craved was rest. Not that I dared tell him that.

'"So I thought I would invite some of my friends over here. Have a nice late Saturday lunch instead of a Sunday one. You know you do such a good roast," he continued, feigning affection as he squeezed my shoulders and gave me that warm smile of his.

'Silly me, I thought that show of affection was real.

'"I'll give you a lift to the shops, can't have you carrying a heavy bag of groceries as well as our baby now, can I?" he said. But, Mary, I could hardly believe what I was hearing and I began to think maybe what he'd said in the hospital about turning over a new leaf just might be true.

'"There's a football match a group of us want to watch but I can't see any point in staying at the pub when we have this new TV here," he said, thinking of his latest purchase, which covered half of the sitting-room wall.

'I didn't have the courage to tell him why I couldn't make myself feel much enthusiasm about that lunch. It was not as though his group of football fan friends were bringing their girlfriends or wives along with them. No, I would have to feed a group of beer-filled men, who would not be lifting many of their fingers to help me. What he seemed unaware of was that I still felt heavy, clumsy even, and so very tired that I longed just to curl up in bed. Lifting anything was painful and taking roasting tins out of the oven would be really difficult. If I could only manage an hour or two of sleep, but I knew better than to say that. Instead, with a sinking heart I managed to keep my smile in place as I agreed to go with him.

'He responded with a warm smile and another hug. Which was all it took to make me lean against him and feel that if cooking dinner for his friends pleased him that much, then I was going to make as much of an effort as I could. Even if that meant having to say goodbye to my much-looked-forward-to afternoon rest.

'"Oh, and Ava, just one more thing, it would be good if you can feed Jade before we get back. Don't want you having to disappear in the middle of the meal now, do we?"

'I managed to stop myself from saying, "That's not really how babies work, they get fed on demand – theirs, not ours." It might have been that request that irritated me slightly but I refused to let it go.

'"Oh, and while you're in the supermarket, I'll pop over to the off licence and get some beers."

'"How many are coming?" I asked him.

'"Oh, only three, but they've big appetites," he said with another grin.

'As this was the first time in ages that Dave had invited friends over, even though it was a warm day, I decided I was going to cook his favourite meal of roast beef and onion gravy.

I was only too aware that the sort of friends he had would tuck in to fish and chips when they were out, but they would expect good red meat when they were invited to our house. Of course they would be after a dessert as well. Apple tart and creamy custard would be popular, I thought.

'So, I scribbled down my shopping list, popped Jade in her sling and let him drop both my son and me off at the supermarket. By the time we returned and all the things I had chosen were in the kitchen, my back was already aching. I sighed at the thought of all the cleaning and cooking I had agreed to do, which was only going to make it worse but keeping the good mood between us was even more important so I'd best do Dave proud and get on with it.

'"My mates will be bringing over some beers as well, so make sure there's enough space in the fridge for them, won't you?" he told me. Then, giving me one of his light slaps on the bottom, he ambled out as if he hadn't a care in the world, while I was left to do all the cooking and cleaning.

'Luckily, our flat is a garden one so I was able to tell Justin to play outside while I vacuumed and that he couldn't watch TV that day. I had to tidy up as well – Dave hadn't done a thing while I'd been in hospital. I quickly told Justin that I wanted to make everything look nice for his dad's friends: "We don't want to get him in a bad mood now, do we?" That one question was enough to stop him arguing.

'"No, Mum," he agreed.

'"Well then, out you go," I said, and handing him a couple of sweets to make him more cheerful, I began tidying. I did feel a bit guilty about reminding him of his father's bad temper as well as stopping him from watching his favourite Saturday morning children's show but I only had so much time to get everything done well enough to satisfy Dave.

'Even though all the windows were open it was one of those muggy days where, with no breeze, the heat in the flat was already making my hair stick to the back of my neck. I just wished that I could go back to bed with a book and a cool drink. Instead I prepared all the food for the main course and made the pastry for my apple tart. When everything was in the oven, I fed Jade before I showered and slipped into a cotton dress, dried my hair and put on some make-up.

'Dave and his three friends, carrying boxes of lager, arrived just as I walked back into the kitchen.

'"Match is almost starting," he announced after briefly introducing me to them, though I can't remember any of their names now. They all looked flushed from the time they had been in the pub and I wondered just how much alcohol Dave had consumed.

'"Can you put those lagers in the fridge, love?" he asked, pointing to the ones he had placed on the floor. And then he pulled out an armful of lagers that had already been chilling before disappearing into the sitting room with his friends.

'I tried in vain to close my ears to the intrusive sound of a TV turned up to full blast and the shouts punctuating the air at every goal scored; shouts that increased in volume as the cans of lager decreased.

'At half-time Dave stumbled into the kitchen to help himself to more beers from the fridge. I suddenly felt nauseous because he was drinking enough to send him into one of his rages.

'No, *he wouldn't*, I thought, *not in front of his friends. Or would he? It would spoil his image if he did*. So, pushing that thought aside, I gave Justin his lunch but I couldn't stop my mind from trying to work out how much drink Dave was knocking back: *was it enough to change his mood, no matter who was there?*

'I felt some relief as the cheers coming from the sitting room at the end of the match told me it was the team they supported that had won. The four men trooped into the kitchen, sniffing the air appreciatively as they helped themselves to more lagers.

'"Mmm, smells good," they all said.

'"Yes, she's a good cook," said Dave with something like pride in his voice.

'The visitors carried everything into the dining area for me, while Dave took in the lagers and placed them on the table. I felt my face flush with pleasure on hearing his praise though I was none too happy to see just how much more lager had been taken to the table. I eyed them nervously. Dave hadn't been drunk since I came back from the hospital but I could see that he was far from sober already – I just hoped that eating would sober him up.

'Seeing I was looking rather hot, it was one of Dave's friends who held out a can of lager to me. When I began to shake my head, he said encouragingly, "Go on, one won't do you any harm – it will cool you down."

'"Don't you be offering drink to Ava, it's not good for her," Dave told him firmly before I had a chance to say that I couldn't drink while I was breastfeeding.

'"I can answer for myself, Dave," I said sharply. As soon as those words had left my mouth, I wanted to suck them back. Too late, I saw the glint in his eyes as he stared at me and his body began to stiffen with temper.

'His friend, sensing the sudden frost in the atmosphere he had caused, wanted to smooth things over quickly and said, "You're a lucky man, Dave, having a woman who can cook like Ava. Nothing out of tins on this table." But then he made his second mistake, giving me a warm friendly smile. One that annoyed Dave even more. He didn't like men paying me attention, not even his friends. Perhaps realising he was embarrassing everyone, Dave managed to pull himself together, leant over the table, took my hand and said they were right, everything looked wonderful.

'There were smiles all round as everyone, including me, relaxed.

'It must have been around then that I heard Jade crying. No doubt their loud voices had woken her up. Excusing myself from the table, I walked into the bedroom.

'A little flushed face told me she needed feeding and changing. Once that was done, I sat on the edge of the bed and rocked her gently until she settled down. Then I looped her carrier over my head and placed her in it. It only took a few more minutes until her breathing grew heavier as she fell asleep on my chest.

'Dave's friends were still eating and drinking when I returned to the table. Dessert plates were being scraped clean and more praise came my way. Coffee was refused, as looking at their watches, they told me they had some more mates to meet up with.

'"Wonderful meal, Ava, thanks for letting us come," the trio said in unison.

'"Make him do the washing up," one of them joked, giving me a playful wink. I said something like I might and smiled at him although of course I knew there was no question of Dave helping. He never did things like washing up, Mary. You know he wasn't that sort of man.'

'So, what happened after they left, Ava?' she urged.

Taking a deep breath, I continued to tell her about that day.

'I glanced over at my good-looking partner, wishing for once he would just make that offer while his mates were there. There were darting pains stabbing through my lower back and what felt like a band was tightening round my head. I really needed a rest.'

'"Well, mate, if you finish your chores in time, we might see you before closing," they joked as, laughing, they made their way out.

'As I shut the door after them, I saw Dave's smile vanish. Those tell-tale twitches of the edge of his mouth and the way he had clenched his face told me I was in real trouble. *Oh God, no*, was the silent scream spinning in my head when I saw the venom in his eyes. I tried to move away from him. I didn't see that his fists had also clenched as his eyes followed me. Any peace that might have been between us was gone. He chose his usual method of causing pain, grabbing hold of my hair and pulling it so hard that once again I was up on my toes.

'"So, you enjoyed disrespecting me in front of my friends, did you? You want them to think I'm a pussy, doing your bidding?" he whispered roughly in my ear in that deceptively quiet voice of his, which was more frightening than his bellowing shouts of rage. "Ava, you are never to show me up in front of my friends again, do you understand? Tell me what you mustn't do?"

'"Not show you up in front of your friends," I repeated.

'"That's a good girl, you're learning," he said and still with that tell-tale twitch, he yanked my hair again. And then he let go. For a moment, I thought it was over.'

'But it wasn't, was it, Ava?' She looked me in the eye as she lifted her head from jotting down notes.

'No, he caught hold of me by the neck, whispering in my ear that he hadn't finished with me yet. He accused me of flirting with his friends. I tried to say I wasn't but he had entered his own world and could no longer hear me. "Are you sure that brat of yours is mine?" he asked and that's when I was really frightened. "Of course she's yours," I told him, trying to keep as calm as I could, despite shaking with fear, "I mean, who else's would she be?" He said there was no telling with me and that I'm at home all day. "So I wonder who's been calling round. Explain then why she's come out so white, why she didn't come out dark like her brother?"

'I tried desperately to find the words to explain that mixed-race children can be of all different shades, but he wasn't interested. "I think you're lying, Ava," he shouted and that's when his fists came fast and furious as he really laid into me. They smashed into my face repeatedly and I could taste the blood in my mouth; it dripped onto the sling and Jade. Then he threw me onto the ground. I managed to twist myself so I didn't fall on the baby – it might have killed her if I had. But he was so far gone, he didn't care who he hurt. You know what saved my life?'

'No.'

'Lager! He'd drunk so much of it, he had to rush to the loo for a pee. He never thought that I would be able to get up and through that door as fast as I did. It was fear for my daughter that gave my feet wings. He was only inches away from me when I slammed the door in his face and screamed for help.'

'Your neighbours and the doctor said you were shouting that he was going to kill you.'

'Well, this time I thought he just might.'

'Ava, do you know how many women in your age group are killed by the men they see as their partners?'

'No.'

'Two a week. Frightening, isn't it? And how many are beaten to the extent that every part of their body is damaged?'

'Tell me?'

'Over a million last year. And how many women still go back to them?'

'I don't know.'

'Too many and they are often the ones who eventually turn up dead. That's the war police officers like me are facing. Not only getting women like you into a place of safety, but also trying to get you all to understand why you should never go back to a man who has beaten you even if they only did it once. It might not have been today, or even tomorrow, but one day he won't stop at blackening your eyes or splitting your lip. And then it might not be a hospital you're taken to, it could just be the mortuary.'

Mary told me very firmly then that if I wanted a peaceful and safe life, not just for me but my children as well, I would have to get sole custody. Which was one of the reasons, she explained, that my cuts and bruises had been photographed. They had taken photos of my blood-splattered infant too. 'Men like him try every trick in the book to torment women who leave them, such as making sure they have rights to see their children, which means they have your address.'

I shuddered at the thought. Somewhere in my mind something clicked and I lifted my head and looked her straight in the eyes. My voice when I spoke was stronger, firmer and more determined: 'I want him out of my life, I have to, I know what you're saying is right,' I told her.

'Good, I know who he is. Your man certainly has a bad reputation. A drug dealer who doesn't care one iota who he sells it to. But then you know that, don't you?'

'Yes,' I whispered.

'But you didn't when you met him?'

'No.'

'Well, I do believe you've made up your mind not to go back this time. With a man like him, there's no friendly way of dealing with your situation. Whatever happens, do not contact him or let him have your address. Even if you got a restraining order it doesn't always stop men like him. Are you prepared to stick to that?'

'Yes.'

'Well then, the next thing we have to sort out is a little easier: getting your belongings out of the home.'

'I've not got much,' I told her, 'and I haven't got my keys either.'

'Look what my partner just dropped in when she came for your son,' Mary said with a wide grin as she dangled his set of keys in front of me. 'We got them when he was searched.'

I told her then that I would rather lose everything than go through that door again.

'Thought you might say that. I can send someone to pick up what you need so make a list. Think clothes for you all, toys, nappies and things like that, also any documents like passports, birth certificates, special photos or jewellery. Just put everything on your list. Even make-up and perfume, a laptop, phone if you have one and the chargers too.'

She passed over a couple of sheets of paper and a pen.

'Are you allowed to do that, use his keys to go in?'

'It's your home too and I seem to remember you asked me to do that for you so the answer is yes. I'll have everything brought round to the place that my colleague has arranged for you to stay in. I'll also be contacting the council on your behalf. They'll do their best to find a home for you and your children. Might take a while, but find one they will. One that is nowhere near where you've been living. I'll leave it up to them to contact you.'

The police officer brought Justin back into the room. I felt relieved that at least he was smiling. 'Time for you and your family to get settled in now,' she told me gently as she took me and the children out to where an unmarked car was waiting.

A young woman was in the driving seat and smiled as the back door was opened.

'Marlene is taking you and the children to the refuge now. I wish you all the best for the future,' Mary said before taking my hand. 'It's all up to you now, Ava.'

I felt the tears welling up; she had been so kind.

'Right,' said my driver, 'we're on our way now.'

Turning round slightly so that I could give a very grateful thank-you wave goodbye, I saw Mary had already disappeared into the station.

2

The evening was still warm and humid, even though I could see the sun's yellow globe disappearing behind the rooftops as we drove through the part of the town where empty shops had boarded-up windows. On one or two of the street corners stood dimly lit pubs, their peeling paint and faded signs adding to the feeling that we were going through an impoverished town.

We passed the rundown shopping centre where the only cinema had been transformed into a bingo hall, before turning into a road where the front doors of the grey stone houses opened straight onto the pavement. Not a tree or a bush in sight, nor even a few people walking to and from their homes. Just a few cars that looked as though they had seen better days. The only sign of life was the presence of a blue light shining through some of the curtains, indicating someone was watching TV.

Another turning and the houses changed again. Built in the sixties with bay-fronted windows, a patch of grass to the front and a garage at the side, they appeared to be the homes of people a lot more affluent than the ones in the roads we had just driven through.

'We're here, Ava,' Marlene announced as she pulled up in front of one such house.

The first thing I noticed was the high and sturdy dark wood fence with an equally thick door at its centre. I could see it had a brass letter box and a bell, where just underneath a small, discreet oblong box had been placed. *No getting to the front door of that house easily*, I thought, feeling more than a little relieved. I noticed Marlene hadn't pressed the bell. Instead her fingers were moving just underneath the box's covering: 'That's a code I'm pressing. It opens the gate and tells whoever's on duty that someone is coming in. It's Denise tonight and she's expecting us. I'll let her explain all about the codes and why they have them here once you get inside.'

As we walked up to the front door it swung open and light spilled out onto the path as Denise, a slim, dark-haired woman with exceptionally bright grey eyes that I felt were assessing me, greeted us. She gave me a warm and welcoming smile and said, 'Hello, Ava. You're safe now so do come on in.'

'I've got to get back to the station,' Marlene told her, 'but I'll be coming over later with Ava and the children's belongings – we've done a list.'

I saw an amused look float onto Denise's face. She must have known exactly how Marlene and Mary were going to collect our things. After all, those who flee from danger hardly stop to pack.

After Marlene had said her goodbyes and told me I was going to be in excellent hands, Denise led me into the duty office. Jade was asleep and Justin had been moved to a small play area, although by now he looked ready for bed. She asked a few questions, more about the children's needs than anything else; she then quickly covered the rules of the refuge, which were the same as Mary and Marlene had already explained, although she did emphasise one other point very strongly. She said of course the women residents chatted to each other, which was good – it helped to get things off their chests: 'But one thing I tell newcomers is to listen, but not ask questions about anything personal, such as where they lived before they came here or what happened that made them seek help.'

'I understand,' I said, 'because it's true, we don't like intrusive questions and especially not from strangers. Who does?'

'Exactly, Ava. Women who are damaged only want to confide in people when they're ready, not have information squeezed out of them. Also, and I think you probably already know this, in most cases it's important that no one knows which town they've come from, or the name of the person responsible for them coming here.'

The final thing Denise told me was that everyone who goes out of the house must have a phone with them: 'We've had some old ones donated to us and on them is the direct number to the police station. That makes everyone feel a little more secure.'

'The police will bring mine here,' I told her, 'and Mary explained the rules to me at the station – they sound pretty easy to stick to.'

'Good, I'll take you to your room now – your son looks as though he's nearly asleep already. I'll show you round the house once you've got him tucked into bed and then we can have a proper chat. I've got a rather small box room for you but we've managed to put in a camp bed and a small cot so at least you'll have some privacy. Everyone else has to share though. For once we're not completely full here but no doubt that will change in a couple of days.

'Oh, and here's a T-shirt your son can sleep in tonight – I don't think he'll stay awake till all your things arrive. Did the police give you an emergency pack? Great, let's show you the bathroom and your room, so you can get him down immediately.'

She was right: Justin's eyes were firmly closed within minutes of me peeling off his clothes and pulling the T-shirt over his head. I hugged him tightly and stroked his cheek, but as I whispered to him that everything would be all right now, I was all too aware that he had not spoken a word since I had run out of the house with Jade. He climbed into bed and was asleep within minutes. The camp bed took up nearly all the floor space between the bed and the cot, but I didn't see bedding that was well-worn or a room that was cramped, what I saw was a clean and warm, cosy cocoon, where for once I could sleep without fear.

My son's heavy breathing told me he was not going to wake until the morning. I just hoped that after everything he had gone through over the last few hours, he would not be plagued by unsettling nightmares. Jade though was wide awake now and wriggling around, letting me know it was nappy changing time again, which I quickly sorted before sitting on the bed and feeding her. Then, not wanting to leave her in the cot till I went to bed, I tucked her back in her carrier and went down to the small cubbyhole that Denise called her office.

'Right, I'll quickly show you around. I told the women that you and your children were arriving today and they have saved you some supper. They're pretty good cooks, I have to say.' She then walked me through the house, pointing out that all the rooms were bedrooms apart from another small one, where a washing machine and cleaning equipment and a small fridge were housed.

'Now I understand you're breastfeeding?'

'Yes.'

Denise explained that all provisions had been made for nursing mothers: 'The fridge in here is for women who are breastfeeding, they can place their expressed milk in there.' She also told me that all the groceries were delivered; that the group of women she had in now took turns in doing the cooking and then she said that the present group of women were all Muslim: 'So, bacon for breakfast is totally out,' she added with a smile. She went on to say that at the moment, I was the only woman with children in the house: 'Though it's a bit unusual, we normally have a few. Shame, really – I expect your son would have liked someone to play with. Anyhow, here's the community room, so let's go and meet the others.'

Denise opened the door for us to walk in. Inside, a cooking area took up about a third of the space and there were a few armchairs, a Formica-covered table, a sagging settee and a small, old TV in the corner.

Pairs of eyes turned in my direction before all four women stood up to greet me as Denise made the introductions. The woman I thought was most probably the eldest by a few years told me her name was Fareeda, the second one was Amira, then the smallest one in the group said, 'Hello, Ava, I'm Farah,' and the last one introduced herself as Ayesha. There was no expression of shock on any of their faces when they saw my battered and swollen one but then I was to learn that they had all seen bruised reflections in their own mirrors. Instead they exclaimed over my baby, cooing what a little angel she was, and then almost as one voice, they said that they expected Justin and I were hungry. They told me they had cooked more than enough for two extras and hoped we were up to joining them a little later. Farah said that it was the rule of the house to always be prepared to welcome a newcomer.

Hunger was something I had given little thought to up until then. Perhaps it was because there was something about the other women's friendliness that almost instantly made me feel better, or maybe it was the tantalising aroma of herbs and spices coming from a couple of pots on the stove that had woken my taste buds.

'You know what? I really am,' I told them gratefully.

The one who had introduced herself as Amira looked pleased. 'Good, because we have plenty and there's a little dessert as well – a sort of cake from my home country. It will be ready for you in two minutes.' With that, she walked over to the stove.

Denise was right: the women were really good cooks.

That evening, it was a vegetarian meal with what they called an upside-down rice cake. I asked what was in it that gave the cake such a distinctive sweet and sour taste.

'Pomegranate syrup,' Amira explained. 'Though at home we usually put in ground walnuts as well. But we don't ask the refuge for them, they are just too expensive. We try and eat mainly vegetarian food because halal meat does cost more and we know a lot of people are against it, but we do cook chicken some evenings. If we had known you were coming sooner, we could have asked for someone to have got a few portions.'

'Don't worry about me, this is all just great,' I told them truthfully.

Farah, who until she explained a couple of things I had thought was wearing some type of long black dress, told me while I was finishing my supper that when she came to the refuge, the first thing she had asked for was a pair of scissors: 'It was a really horrible burka I had on until I cut off the part that covers our heads and most of our faces. Now it's just a horrible dress,' she said with a grin.

It was she, who after I had eaten every scrap of the meal, observed, 'You look very tired, Ava. I think you need a good night's sleep.'

'Not with a baby that needs feeding every few hours,' I answered with a wry smile.

'Still, some chamomile tea will do you good, help you relax,' she told me as she put the kettle on. 'Just let it steep for a few minutes then take it up with you – you'll find it really calming.'

'And here's some ointment,' Amira said, pressing a small jar into my hand. 'It will help get that swelling down.'

Which was the closest any of them came to mentioning my bruising.

Holding a large mug of aromatic herbal tea, I climbed the stairs up to my bedroom and what I told myself was to be my first peaceful night in a long time.

3

So, what did I learn from that refuge apart from some more about babycare and cooking? That a group of women who bond will always look out for each other – it's their togetherness that gives them strength. It helps them draw back their shoulders, look people in the eye and say, 'No, we're not victims, we are survivors.' Believing that gives them the motivation and confidence to walk away from their old lives before stepping briskly into new ones.

Then there were the other things we really should have known about, but none of us did until it was much too late. That sooner or later a man who intentionally begins to strip a woman of her independence will raise his fists to her. And the final thing was to have only people in our immediate circle that we are certain we can trust. For example, we all knew how careful we must be while in the refuge. We had to trust each other that we would all obey the rules there because they were not just there for one person, they were there for all of us and all those who would need the refuge after we left. And letting anyone know how to find the refuge was the very worst rule to break because doing so could put other women's lives in danger.

And every woman in there with me knew that.

* * *

It was Farah I found myself most drawn to. Underneath that long, baggy dress of hers, she was a tiny little thing. She had deep green eyes and a mop of thick dark blonde hair not to mention a rather dry sense of humour, which she was beginning to be able to show, but what impressed me most was the gentleness in the way that she smiled and looked at me and my children. I also sensed a deep sadness in her. When I first met her, she had appeared rather shy and it took me a while to understand it was not so much shyness as shame that she had ended up in the refuge; a sense that she should have been able to take control of her life. *How did it happen?* she asked me – which was the same question I had put to myself on countless occasions. Her unhappiness was caused not so much by a marriage that had clearly failed, but by how much she was missing the part of her family who had left the UK not long after her wedding. Though she didn't tell me where they had gone to, not then, but that detail came later.

In fact, there were snippets of information in everyone's conversation. Enough to tell me that some dreadful things had happened to them. Not only that, whereas I was not really scared about going outside, they definitely were. Even the phones that had been given to them with the direct line to the police on speed dial did not seem to make them feel any more secure. I knew they were trying hard to leave their past behind and kept the conversation around clothes and cooking.

Amira, who was dressed in a pair of baggy trousers and a man's shirt, told us that the clothes she was wearing when she was brought to the refuge had been ripped in places so she had been given these ones, which she wore every day.

'People donate things,' she explained. 'Clothes, shoes and those phones we all have, they have been given by kind people who try and help women they have never met. I'm waiting for a small, kind person who wants to clear her wardrobe out and send it here – can't wait to be out of this hideous dress and wearing something nice!'

A little burst of laughter broke out at these comments.

'You'll have first choice when the next lot of clothes are donated,' the others told her kindly. 'Good thing we're not all the same size.'

It seemed I was the lucky one, having all my own clothes brought over to me even though there were only a few changes in the suitcase and pyjamas for Justin and me. Then again, no questions were asked about how I had managed that, any more than I asked how the others hadn't been so lucky.

4

It was while I was taking my turn at cleaning the kitchen that Denise appeared to tell us she was expecting a new arrival.

Farah had protested when I offered to do my share. She said I had enough to do looking after my baby and feeding every few hours. Besides, she had noticed my stiffness and realised that my body must still be sore from childbirth: 'So shouldn't you be resting when you have the chance?'

I told her it was something I wanted to do; that I was keen to keep busy and moving around a little would stop me from getting too stiff.

'Anyhow, I've been here three days and done nothing,' I added, 'while you and the others have been doing all the cooking and cleaning.'

'See you're doing a good job here,' Denise said to me with a smile – she must have heard some of Farah's comments. There was very little that passed her.

'Well, my partner was rather fussy,' was all I said, but I guess she must have had a shrewd idea of just what happened to me if I left even an unwashed cup out.

She didn't say anything about the woman who was arriving, just dropped a hint for us to make her feel welcome. Yet I sensed she was not completely happy about the newcomer. Later that morning, when I was having a coffee break, Denise brought her into the communal room to meet us. Tall, with flaming bottle-red hair, wearing the tightest jeans possible and a sleeveless top, she was, I could see, covered in bruises; a nasty row of them around her neck spoke volumes. Some of the bruises were old ones which had faded to a pale yellow, others so fresh that they were still coming out.

I wondered why she was wearing a sleeveless top, for I could also see the puncture marks on her arms and I was pretty sure that Denise had spotted them as well. Which would have explained why I had felt she was uneasy about this woman. Still, Denise introduced us to Bella – as we were told her name was.

* * *

Unlike the other women, with whom I already felt a kinship, discretion was not a word in Bella's vocabulary. That first evening, she talked nonstop about her beatings, saying the man she had just left was 'proper scary. A no-good bastard who almost never worked'. Luckily for us, she enjoyed listening to music on her headphones that were attached to a little player. At least that gave us a break from hearing all the episodes of her life story when we were all together in the kitchen/living area. Not that she made any effort to offer help. Instead she moaned constantly about not being able to have bacon sandwiches for breakfast: 'I'll have to go out and get them,' she said as though not having them in the refuge was a real ordeal.

'Oh, I'm not that worried about going out,' she declared when she asked where we went and was told that none of us had been outside since we had come in. 'I suppose that's not so surprising; hardly think you want to show your face around, Ava. And I suppose you lot are used to not being let out unless you're walking three steps behind a man,' she added, tossing her head in the direction of the other women. I suppose the Muslim women must have been more used to derogatory remarks like that than they should have been, for on hearing them, they just stared at her blankly and said nothing.

Still, the good bit was that Bella proved true to her word: she only had some tea for breakfast and then disappeared for hours each day. Her absence certainly pleased me for she was someone I really wanted to steer clear of. She, on the other hand, seemed to want to talk to me whenever we bumped into each other. As for the rule of not asking questions, she broke that one every time she opened her mouth. And when she wasn't asking personal questions, she was complaining about anything she could think of – one constant being about Jade's crying waking her up in the night.

'Can't you stick a dummy in her mouth? That's what I'd do to shut the brat up' was another comment that received no response from me.

As well as not enjoying her company one bit, there was also something about Bella that was making me feel really nervous. I couldn't tell what it was, maybe the watchful expression in her eyes when she had fired questions at me, the main ones being the name of my partner, or 'man', as she called him. Or it might just have been my instinctive sense of self-preservation. Although she may have been badly beaten herself, that didn't stop Bella from being bad news for the equilibrium at the refuge. Especially when she dropped out the fact that she had two children.

'So where are they?' I asked curiously.

'Oh, social took them away,' she told me with a nonchalant shrug. 'Said there was a lot to be sorted out before we could talk about their future. I mean, they're worried I might go back to my boyfriend, a right dangerous fucker.'

I could feel the shock coming from the other women in the kitchen and I don't think it was just her language that caused this – more likely her lack of interest in her children had robbed them of words.

'Anyhow, better for you if there are no more of them noisy little brats in here, isn't it? Not that your boy ever says anything, I reckon he's not normal.'

And with that proclamation, she walked out.

5

Bella appeared to be putting out a message that she didn't care in the least whether we liked her or not, although I sensed some of her act was partly bravado. Those bruises on her arms were where strong fingers had grabbed hold of her, likewise the yellow ones on her neck told me that she had been half-choked before being let go to fall on the floor. Yes, those were marks I recognised all too well, which is why I could visualise exactly how she had come by them. They were also the ones she showed off as much as possible, as if she was saying, *I don't care* – but I'm sure she did. There was an anger in her and not being able to take it out on the man who was the very reason she was in the refuge, she let her rage escape in our direction. It was that which partly stopped me feeling sorry for her – it was clear she didn't have an ounce of compassion for those who had suffered too. Not to mention the fact that she was downright rude to the women at the shelter.

Another one of her faults that got on my nerves was the way she appeared to take delight in complaining about the rules: 'Can't see why I can't have a friend visiting me. Not like any of my mates would drop me in it by giving out the address.'

'It's the rule and a very sensible one,' I said, trying not to let my annoyance show, 'or at least it makes sense to me,' I added abruptly.

She went quiet then, most probably thinking that if I was not going to agree with her then I might just report her. And that could mean her ending up outside of the refuge.

'I've noticed you don't go out either,' she said, meaning that she was the only one who wanted to venture out. A comment that was true and one I didn't bother giving an explanation to. I just couldn't bring myself to say that she might not mind walking around showing off all her bruises clearly given to her by clenched fists, but I certainly did.

The police officer Marlene who had driven us to the refuge had done as she had promised, dropping off everything I had asked for, plus a few other bits and pieces of make-up that she had assumed were mine so I had my own clean clothes to wear, as had Justin and Jade, as well as an assortment of games and picture books. While still not talking, my son did immerse himself in games and loved snuggling close to me as we looked at the books together. As a result, we had a bedroom floor that could hardly be seen.

But with those bruises on my face that had only just begun to fade a little, I was still nervous about leaving the refuge. No one likes to be stared at, do they? On the other hand, I felt I would have to get over that, if only for the sake of my son. Poor little mite, even with his games and books, he was getting so bored. Although there was a decent-sized garden at the back of the house, there was nothing for him to play on. He was used to being taken to parks where there were swings and slides, as well as other children he could join up with. The women in the refuge went out of their way to help me with my two. They offered to look after Jade when I wanted some time for a shower and encouraged Justin in drawing pictures, although I hate to think what sort of images might have been in his head.

That must have been the only time that Bella showed any interest in him: 'Try and draw your mum and dad,' she suggested, holding out a couple of crayons to him.

But Justin simply shook his head and I understood the reason, which made me really sad. Of course he didn't want to think about his dad or remember the last time he had seen him. He must have tried very hard to block that out of his memories for he hadn't uttered a single word since that day.

'Doesn't talk, does he? Bit backward, is he?' Bella asked.

Boy, I wanted to slap her for that remark but I managed to say, 'Not at the moment, he's just shy.'

Thankfully, she said nothing more and walked away.

* * *

What I should do, I began telling myself, is start to reconnect with a few of my old and trusted friends. The ones I must have upset by dropping them once Dave gained control of me. One name flew into my head: an old friend that I felt would understand what had happened, and if we met, wouldn't spend all her time quizzing me. I just wasn't ready to talk about Dave and what had gone so wrong. Although she might be a bit annoyed that I hadn't been in touch, I plucked up the courage and gave her a call. To my relief, instead of accusing me of dropping her, she simply said, 'Hi Ava, I wondered when you would phone me. Sounds like you must have left him?'

'Yes,' was all I managed to say.

'Well, thank goodness for that. I knew from the moment I met him it was all charm on the outside and pure bad on the inside. But that's yesterday, isn't it? So, where are you?'

'Um, I can't give you the address.'

'Oh, say no more! You're in a refuge, aren't you? And I can guess why that is. Just tell me which town. I gather it's not the other end of England?'

'No, just enough of a distance away from Dave,' I explained as I gave her the name of the town.

'Oh, that's a bus journey away for me, so no problem,' she said lightly. 'Let's make it tomorrow, shall we? I'll find out where there's a cafe we can meet and message you the address, OK?'

'Sounds good and I forgot to tell you: I have two children now, one's still a small baby.'

'Mmm, we can chat about all of that when we meet. We have a lot of catching up to do.'

*　*　*

When I finished the call, I felt that I had made my first positive step towards being back in control of my life. I was really looking forward to meeting Jean. Not that Jean is her real name. She's had more than enough publicity in various newspapers, so I've changed it. I could hardly believe that it had been nearly five years since we had last seen each other. She was another friend that Dave had persuaded me to drop. Which didn't mean that I hadn't missed her; not only that, I felt ashamed of myself for not being there for her when she needed friends around her the most. The last time I had seen her, she had still been trying to put her life back together. Like me, she had been in a relationship that over time slid quickly from bad to beyond bad. Like me, the romance in her relationship died abruptly as he turned into a violent and jealous man who had no ear at all for reason. As she said the last time we met, if only she had left him the first time he hit her, maybe things would have turned out differently.

Jean had gone through a court case where she had fought for sole custody of her children, a boy and a girl, and won. Never an easy thing to do. For her partner had told her how he loved his kids and had begged her to give him another chance. Something that she was strong enough to say no to.

She had been moved by the council into a place of her own. One that he had not been given the address of and she thought it was far enough away from the area they had lived in. But it hadn't taken him long to find out where she and their children were living. And once he found it, within days, both their names were splashed across the newspapers.

The story that was released stated that she had been in an abusive relationship for years. And there was no mistaking the fact that after he lost custody of his children, he had planned to kill both Jean and them. Whether what happened was intentional or not is a question that can never be answered, the TV newsreader stated. It seemed that it was similar to what we see sometimes see in crime films. The ones where specially trained police try to talk the man into putting his gun or his knife down. Though in this case it was a shotgun; not something the public expect to see in real life. One that he was clutching as he marched in the direction of where Jean and her children were living.

I should think that the people who saw him striding past purposefully could hardly believe their eyes. Luckily, it shocked more than one of them enough to call the police and tell them exactly where they had seen him and the direction in which he was heading. It didn't take long for an army of police to work out where he was going. They reached Jean's house more or less at the same time as he did. He had only got as far as the gate but not inside it. The police used a megaphone to warn Jean and the children who were standing behind her to stay away from the windows as they surrounded him. Wearing bulletproof jackets and armed themselves, they ordered him to stay where he was. They were aware of why the restraining order was issued and that he had made more than one threat to kill all his family. Jean had always denied that he would have carried through with this: 'He's just screwed up,' she kept saying, somehow convincing herself that she knew that in his own way he still loved them and would never harm his children.

So, who knows what his intentions really were that day.

The ending was tragic enough. For hours it seemed the police tried to talk him into putting the gun down: 'Just put the gun down on the ground,' they said. Jean always thought that he was growing tired when he made what seemed to be a movement to place the gun where he had been asked. Just as it seemed as if it was all over, the gun went off, firing straight up into his chest, near his heart. The police rushed forward, tried to stem the bleeding, while a sobbing, hysterical Jean came rushing out. The paramedics arrived. Too late, he was dead, they said; his body was covered before being placed in the ambulance.

Jean had glanced up then to see two white faces staring out of the window. Her children had just watched their father being killed, even if it was by his own hands.

I cannot think, even if she no longer loved him, what it must have been like to see the body of the man she was once besotted by, the one who had fathered her children, lying dead in front of her. Had he killed himself on purpose? No one knows. She always thought it was suicide; that he couldn't bring himself to be apart from his family since she had gained sole custody of their children. And even though he had beaten her up so badly, she had stopped believing that one day he would stop, she still mourned the fact that he was dead: 'We should have been moved further away so he couldn't find us,' she told me, 'then he wouldn't have known where we were. And he wouldn't have died that day.'

'Of course I'm sad he did that,' she told me later. 'But there was no helping him really. My therapist told me that he would eventually have found another woman and the chances were that she too would have ended up battered, if not dead.'

Although that was true, I still understood then just how much courage it had taken her to leave him.

I hoped that the years since I had last seen her had been

good for Jean and that her children had had the help they must have needed to get over seeing how their father died. At least they must have realised that it was not a police bullet that had ended his life.

Yes, Jean and I had a lot to catch up on.

That night, I went to bed smiling because she had sent me the name of a cafe where we would meet at ten the following day.

*   *   *

That morning, I worked hard at making myself look as presentable as possible. I pulled on jeans and a light blue long-sleeved shirt. That hid a lot. Next, I stared at my reflection in the mirror and I accepted that this was not going to be as easy. *Thank goodness for concealer*, I thought, as I applied as much of it as I could. Luckily the weather was good enough to wear sunglasses so I felt I had at least managed to hide the worst of those bruises.

At breakfast, Farah offered to look after the baby when I told her I was going out to meet an old friend, but I still couldn't bear to let Jade out of my sight. She was completely understanding about that and told me to enjoy being outside. As for Justin, he was just about tugging at my hand when he heard we were going out for a walk.

As the refuge was in a small town quite a few miles from where I had lived with Dave, I was not too scared about putting my feet outside of it. My bruises were not so bad now and I had been able to cover them quite well.

'So, where are you off to then?' Bella asked when she saw I was going out.

What I wanted to say was mind your own business, but as Justin was looking at me for the answer as well, I foolishly said, 'Oh, just a cafe.'

'Not many of them round here, hope you find a decent one. Still, have a nice time, you two,' she said.

Forcing myself to give her a friendly smile, I ushered Justin through the door and promptly forgot about the small piece of information I had just parted with so easily.

It was good being outside and feeling free. I had the address Jean had given me on my phone. Not knowing the town, I had asked Denise where it was and she had explained that the cafe was tucked away down a little side street and although it wasn't smart, it had good sandwiches and fabulous homemade cakes as well – 'It's been there for years,' she told me, before reminding me once again to keep the details of the refuge confidential.

It didn't take long to find the place and there was Jean, who jumped up from the table as soon as she saw me and gave me a long and very tight hug. I felt a wave of emotion overtaking me, it was so good to be meeting up with an old friend again.

She certainly looked a lot different than she had the last time I had seen her. Hair well cut, smart clothes freshly ironed and best of all, there were no dark shadows under her eyes. She, on the other hand, could see that I looked pretty worn out.

'I suppose it was him who stopped you seeing me,' she said with a hint of sadness.

'He stopped me seeing just about everyone,' I told her.

She kept looking at Jade. 'She's going to be a little beauty,' she told me. 'And as for Justin, he's a looker too.' She rummaged in her bag and brought out a picture colouring book. 'That's for you, young man,' she told him and received one of his dazzling smiles in return. As soon as she passed over some crayons, he set to work colouring in the pictures, which gave us the opportunity to chat a bit more. A large slice of chocolate cake placed in front of him helped as well, allowing us to talk about what had befallen us since we last met.

One bit of advice that Jean gave me, learnt from all her years of therapy, became lodged in my brain: she encouraged me to spend time going over those years I had been with Dave.

'You've also got to remember who you were before you met him and work at being that person again, only much stronger and a lot wiser.'

'And a little older,' I pointed out ruefully.

'You know what I mean, Ava – you had a job you liked then, your own flat and you were busy putting your life together after what had happened to you earlier. And then he walked in and wrecked everything you had achieved, didn't he? And don't say it was partly your fault either. Blaming yourself is never helpful.'

And I knew that last remark came from what she herself had gone through during those previous years.

'It's funny, isn't it? I knew what Dave was like the moment I met him, but I didn't have a clue when I first met Tom. Anyhow, you wouldn't have listened any more than I did. So, while you're at the refuge, make some notes and contact the people who were your friends before – they will understand, or at least the real ones will. And try to analyse what went wrong. If you're offered therapy, which I'm sure you will be, take it. If not, tell the doctor you are still suffering from the shock of what happened and ask for it firmly.'

We then chatted about our children and how nice it was to meet again.

I felt so much lighter when we walked out of that cafe. At least I was with someone who had known the old me and understood so much of why I had let my life take the wrong turnings. But if I was feeling more relaxed than I had in years, all that disappeared when after walking just a few yards, I heard a voice that made my whole body shake.

'I'm watching you, Ava,' it said.

For a moment I just froze and then forcing myself, I turned slowly round.

And there was Dave, a cold smile on his face.

'You can't take what's mine,' he told me and his hand moved so fast, he had grabbed hold of Justin's arm before what was happening penetrated my mind. He might have thought that I was in a state of shock and unable to move, but he had completely underestimated Jean.

She tore after him, yelling that he was a child molester who had snatched the boy. That stopped him in his tracks as people turned to look at him. They might not want to get involved in most things, but seeing a young boy being abducted is enough to mobilise most bystanders.

'I'm calling the police now,' she screamed, waving her mobile in the air. 'See my fingers are already on the emergency number.'

He turned, glaring at us as I walked as fast as I could towards them with Jade, who on hearing the commotion, began crying.

It was Jean who held her hand out to Justin, who took hold of it gratefully and then came close to her side.

'So, how did you know where to find her, Dave?' Jean asked him.

His response was to laugh and mutter about little birds chattering before he stormed off.

'Right, Ava, I think you need to act now. I was going to leave it till I saw you next to tell you about a solicitor who deals with family law. I'm ringing her now to see if she's free. You don't want to wait a minute longer,' my friend told me.

The call took hardly any time at all as Jean very precisely told whoever was on the end of the line just why I needed that urgent appointment.

'We're lucky, she has a free appointment in five minutes, so stop shaking and let's go.'

Before I could ask any questions, Jean told me that she knew all about this solicitor because she had once worked in the same office as the one she herself had used: 'After I spoke to you yesterday on the phone, I called and asked if she could recommend anyone here and it's this one and she told me she's ace. So, no excuses. Not that you look capable of making any.'

Taking my arm, she walked me up the high street to a small block of offices. She came in with me, taking on the task of keeping Jade and Justin calm while I explained my situation to the receptionist.

With her curly, short auburn hair and casual outfit of jeans and a blue sweater, the solicitor who ushered us in looked pretty young. Within minutes of her talking, I could see just how on the side of women she was, though.

'The police will already have everything we need to get a restraining order,' she advised me. 'Not that one usually stops men like him. I will send in a report, which they can add to theirs about him trying to snatch your son. Great that you managed to catch that on your phone, Jean, and the video will be really useful evidence. Now, it's sole custody we have to get sorted, Ava, and I don't see much of a problem there.'

'Yes, the police have already advised me of that,' I said.

There were more instructions on what I needed to do. The first thing was to talk to the person in charge of the refuge: 'It's important they find out how he knew where you were. You've not told anyone their address or which town you're in, have you?'

'Only Jean knows which town. She's the only one I've talked to and I knew she would understand why we have to be so careful.'

'And trust me, after what I've been through, I know better than to tell a soul,' Jean assured her.

'Yes, you would totally understand that. I remember your case well, Jean.'

Listening to them both talking, a name came into my head of just who it might be. Not that I could accuse her before I was a little more certain, but I really had no doubts.

The meeting ended and I felt reassured that we had a plan of action. Jean and I agreed we would have to find another meeting place next time. Then I walked back to the refuge knowing that all I had to do was tell whoever was in charge that day what had happened and repeat the mocking remark, 'Little birds chatter'. Who had placed the idea in his head to make Dave hang around outside that cafe? That was all Bella knew, but I hoped the refuge would ask to be shown her phone history.

When I returned, I was pleased to see that it was Denise who was on duty that day – I felt I knew her a little more than the others who worked there. She could see I was upset as soon as I said that I needed to talk to her and she sat me down and listened to everything I had to say; she didn't look too happy at the end of that either.

I told her that I thought the only person it could be was Bella.

'What makes you think that?'

But even as Denise put that question to me, I could tell that me saying Bella's name had not surprised her. I told her that she asked too many questions and had kept wanting to know my partner's name. I explained that he's a drug dealer and she was either an addict or now in recovery – 'I'm pretty sure it's the former, she's the only one who disappears for hours. And the last time she came back, she seemed pretty high to me,' I added.

'But where would she have met him? He doesn't live round here.'

'That's true, Denise, but there are no nightclubs here, are there? And that's where dealers hang out. There are two where he lives and that's not far from here, is it?'

'No, it's not. It's the nearest town to us,' she said thoughtfully.

'I should think by now loads of people know about what happened that night when the police dragged him out of the house. The sort of people he mixes with, anyhow. So even if she found a dealer here, they would almost certainly know Dave.'

'Right, I'll talk to her.'

'And here's Dave's phone number,' I told her, writing it down on a scrap of paper. 'If she's been ringing him, that number will be on her phone.'

As it was, Denise didn't even have to look at Bella's phone because the moment I saw her, Bella must have guessed by the expression on my face that I had a good idea who it was who had dropped me in it.

'Denise wants to see you,' was all I managed to say before tears welled up in Bella's eyes and trickled down her face.

'I didn't mean any harm,' she said, trying to place a hand on my arm, 'he just wanted to know if his kids were all right.'

'Don't lie,' I snapped. 'You told him more than that. Anyhow, it's Denise you've got to explain yourself to, not me.' I almost felt sorry for her – I knew all about addiction and how it can change people's behaviour and how they will do anything to get the drug of their choice. 'She's waiting for you, Bella,' I told her firmly, trying not to catch the eyes of any of the other women.

* * *

It was some time later when Denise came into the room and asked if she could have a word with me. She told me that Bella had admitted to telling Dave where I was going but swore she hadn't told him where the refuge was. He had asked her – he knew who she was and that she had been in a refuge before, which is why he managed to single her out and how he knew that her children had been taken away from her.

'So, what's going to happen to her?' I asked, beginning to feel really bad.

'Oh, I'm not throwing her out, but she's agreed to be transferred to another place where they will help with her addiction. She's packing now.'

Without saying any more, I put two and two together and came up with the conclusion that Bella would be taken to rehab. I spoke to her before she left and told her that getting off drugs was her last chance. And no, I wasn't angry with her, just disappointed, but I still wished her luck for she was just another damaged person, trapped by the drugs that put money in the dealers' pockets. Then I reflected on my relationship with Dave and felt guilty that I had stayed with a man who actively wrecked the lives of others but I was already deeply involved with him before I found out how he earned his money. My excuse was that I was still only sixteen when I met him and by the time I found out how he made his money, I was too besotted and too young to really care.

That was another issue I had to face up to if I was going to put my life back in order. Though apart from a short break since my early teens, my life had never really been that way so this was something else I now needed to come to terms with.

6

It was after Bella was gone that I remembered a conversation that had taken place a couple of days after her arrival. We were all gathered in the community room once we had finished our supper and washed up and were pouring out cups of herbal tea.

During the few days I had been there at the refuge I had heard snippets of conversation that told me the other women had left home in such a hurry, they had been unable to bring much with them. Not that I had either. But as the police had turned up and arrested Dave, it had been possible to have all my few personal belongings as well as everything my children needed, collected. So why hadn't someone been able to do the same for them? I had wondered about that. Not that I asked any of them about it, but Bella, who paid scant attention to rules, had.

It was Amira who, in her halting English, explained to us why they hadn't dared report their husbands to the police. Instead they had all contacted an organisation that helped them find a safe place. The reason why they didn't want to report them became clearer that evening. Mainly it was because they were too afraid of being found. If they angered their husbands any more, a huge search for them would take place, led by their husbands and their families. And then they would be in even more danger.

'There are people who know where the refuges are,' Farah added. 'Not everyone who has been in one keeps quiet, do they? And the reason refuges run out of space is because of men; men who believe they rule the world and that us women are second-class citizens. Even if we come from different cultures, all of us in here have experienced some of the same problems.'

It was that conversation that made me feel that their circumstances were even worse than mine. I wondered if their marriages had ever been happy, even at the beginning. At least my relationship had not started off badly and unlike them, I had nothing to fear from Dave's family so I was a lot luckier than the other women there.

Something else I learnt a little later was that they had all been quickly transferred to an area far enough away from where they had been living to make it even harder to find them. Which explained why we had been told not to ask questions. There was always the risk that others in the refuge might let slip where the other women there came from.

Putting those thoughts together made me understand that their situation must have been dire. It made me almost feel ashamed of myself. Because if I hadn't been so downbeat, I could just have packed a suitcase and left, but by then depression hadn't let me think that there was anywhere I could have gone to.

I suppose I should have known better than to end up living with Dave so quickly. But how well had I really known him? I thought I did and that was my mistake. It was when I went back to my room clutching another cup of that calming chamomile tea, and once Justin was asleep and my baby had been fed and changed, that I began to put my thoughts in order.

Just how had I ended up here and how had I stayed with Dave for five years?

It was those questions that made me remember something else Bella had said that evening: 'I'll tell you what those men do, they try and stop us having freedom. They think they own us and we have to do everything they demand. They get jealous if we talk to other men, even if it's just a friend of theirs, don't they? Always accusing us of flirting or even worse, aren't they?'

I think I must have nodded in response to that. Seeing it was Dave's jealousy that had caused him to nearly kill me and Jade. The other women looked a little puzzled, for their culture, they explained, didn't allow them to talk freely with men, but they all agreed about control.

'Yes,' Bella had gone on, 'they even try and stop us going to Christmas work parties, don't they? They don't like the thought that we might be friendly with our colleagues. Those are the early signals all right. And we all know what the next one is, don't we?'

A question that silenced us all for we guessed what she was about to say next.

'Well, what I'm saying is the first time a man raises his fist is never going to be the last time, is it?' Bella had posed the question and we felt her looking at each one of us in turn.

Again, there was silence to that question, for we all knew by then that what she said was true. After all, those warning signals had appeared before Dave turned violent, hadn't they? I just refused to see them. In the early stages of our being together, I was completely infatuated. Infatuated enough not to see the signs of him trying to control me. But it wasn't locked doors or raised fists that made me a prisoner, it was charm and affection. Dave really had me convinced that he had the same feelings for me as I had for him. Which meant that I never questioned any of his actions, which were subtle enough to begin with.

The demanding ones came later. Like he didn't tell me to drop my friends, it was just that when I told him I'd been invited on a girls' night out, he managed to look a little upset.

'Oh, I wish I'd known earlier! I'd arranged for us to go out and meet up with a few of my friends. Wanted to show you off a little ...'

So, I cancelled my arrangement.

Then there was the odd work do, which I had always enjoyed as it made me feel part of the team. I was just applying a little make-up in the office loo when one of the girls, all round-eyed and grinning, rushed in to tell me that a gorgeous tall man was waiting for me in reception.

And there he was, all smiles on his face as soon as he saw me: 'I thought I'd take you out for a drink since it's Friday,' he'd said. And did I remind him that I'd told him that I was going out with my work colleagues? No, of course I didn't –

I just made a quick excuse to my friends and sailed out of the door with him.

So that was the beginning of him gaining control. As I said, so far it was all done by using charm to manipulate me but within a year of us being together, one by one I had dropped my friends. Jean had been more or less the first one. OK, she was in a bad state and he appeared sympathetic at first. It took a little time for him to say he was concerned that she was becoming too dependent on me; that she wanted all my attention, which was becoming increasingly demanding on our time together and that he didn't think it was doing me much good so I'd better stand up for myself. So, I began to use pleasant excuses whenever Jean called; ones such as I was out for the day, that sort of thing. Not that I fooled her for long. And that's how my friends, the ones who would later have stood by me when I needed help, slowly disappeared from my life.

By the time he felt there was little I was capable of doing independently, it only took a few more months for him to start showing his dark side. But then, as I had learnt from various conversations with both Bella and Jean, that is how abusive men work: the violent side of them is tucked firmly away until they feel in complete control of a woman's feelings. After all, a thump across the face during the first few weeks of meeting her would make a new girlfriend block him on her phone and never see him again. That's if they didn't go to the police and lay a charge. No, men like him wait until the woman they have chosen is so deeply in love with them, they haven't the willpower to walk away. In fact, they often blame themselves for their partner's burst of temper, or at least make excuses for them. So, not only do they step-by-step cut their friends, family and support systems out of their lives, they even cease socialising with their work colleagues until all the invitations dry up.

Once Dave believed that the first stage of getting me dependent on him was successful, he moved on to the next one: to stop me having a career. After all, earning my own money gave me independence and I didn't have to ask him for cash to buy necessities. Which was just as well, for he didn't always have money. Which I tolerated even though I knew the reason. Not that I let on to him that I did. He was aware that I knew about his drug dealing, but not about his own addiction – gambling. An addiction that although he saw money going down the drain, he couldn't put a halt to. It was my wages from the restaurant where I worked front of house that bought us food and paid the rent by then. Not that I ever complained.

By the time I managed to escape from him, I still couldn't answer the question of why, when he needed the money coming in from me, did he want me to leave my job? A question that after being in the refuge for a few days, I started to realise the answer to. Was he afraid that my boss might notice the black eyes and the scarf worn around my neck even in a heatwave?

Of course the best way to keep their wife or girlfriend grateful that they had someone in their lives was to persuade them to get pregnant. Which is exactly what Dave had done to me. I think about those months when I became too frightened to leave the house. So often I had to try and cover my face with make-up to hide the bruises. There was more than one occasion when he forbade me to go out to the shops – there would have been no escaping the fact that I had been badly beaten if I ventured outside. And there was always the possibility that someone might raise the alarm.

Pretty soon, all the spunk I once had dissipated – I only have a dim memory of the feisty youngster I had once been. Instead of picturing my early days with him when I was the person I wish I had remained, my thoughts of being with Dave now summoned up very different images. I saw myself limping down the road to the shops, constant fear fluttering under my ribs as I prayed that I hadn't been guilty of doing something else that would offend him. I tried to switch my memories of that part of my life off, only to have other, more treacherous ones step up to replace them.

Such as that evening when I had first seen him.

Wow, he's really handsome was the first thought that came into my head the moment I saw a six-foot-tall man with a slim, muscular body, standing at the bar. As he turned slightly, I saw that a lock of blue-black hair had flopped engagingly across his forehead. And then there were those mesmerising deep brown eyes that met mine when he looked in my direction. Those eyes of his would have made every woman in the bar hope that she would be the one he approached.

I really thought I was the lucky one when, within a few moments of noticing me, he walked over to the table where I was sitting with Hazel, a friend who had done much to help me over the last few months. Could he, when he locked eyes with mine, have been able to spot that I was vulnerable? What radar did he have to sense that I had little support in my life and was more or less alone in the world?

I know I was nervous that night, even though I had taken time to make myself look as good as I could. It was the first time in months that I had been able to sit in a wine bar with a friend, especially one who had helped me in several ways. It was thanks to her that for the first time in my life I had my own place to stay in. Not only that, it was she who had helped me find a job and that evening, we were celebrating my first pay packet.

'To a new life,' she said as she toasted me with a glass of sparkling wine.

And that night, I really believed it was a new beginning.

It certainly hadn't taken Dave long to walk over to us and ask if we minded if he joined us for a while.

'Hard to say no, shove off,' Hazel said, laughingly. Though I expect she wished that was exactly what he had done.

Before we actually said yes or no, he had pulled out a seat and sat down on it. He was certainly good at putting people at their ease. Even I relaxed a little, as usually I found it hard to chat to someone I didn't know. And as soon as he saw our glasses were empty, he insisted on buying us a couple of drinks.

'Here, let me,' he said when Hazel started to get up from the table, and ignoring our protests he took hold of our glasses and walked over to the bar. Both Hazel and my mouths nearly dropped open when we saw the conspicuous roll of bank notes he pulled out. Peeling a couple of notes off the roll, he placed an order. I had no idea how he came by it. If I had, I would have run a mile but by the time I did discover how one day he had loads of cash and the next day he had empty pockets, it was far too late to step away.

That night, he certainly put on a great performance. He asked us both what kind of work we did and looked really interested when I told him I was working as a receptionist. What I didn't tell him was that the job was new and down to Hazel for finding it. During our three-way conversation I revealed that I had my own flat – well, to be honest, it was more like a large bedsitter and something else that Hazel had organised for me and it was she who had put down the deposit.

Hazel noticed if I didn't that he hardly gave away anything about himself. Later he said to me that he was really cautious in what he let slip. He just mentioned something vague about import and export when she asked what he did for a living. I suppose looking back on it, that statement did have a kernel of truth in it. By the end of the evening he asked us both for our phone numbers and then with a wink, he was off, leaving me with a thudding heart.

He left it three days before he rang and I was over the moon when he did. So, if anyone asked me how did our relationship start, from me noticing a handsome man and him being aware of it? It was that evening, really.

7

When I had first come into the refuge and been told not to ask questions but to listen, I hadn't given that request much thought but gradually I learnt that telling parts of our stories to each other was beneficial to us all. Though there was one of us, Fareeda, who hardly uttered a word. I remember so clearly the time I came down to the kitchen early in the morning to make myself a cup of tea. She was hunched up in an armchair staring into space, or rather, I guessed, into a past which she had no desire to revisit. Shafts of sunlight coming through the window illuminated the dark shadows under her eyes and the lines on a face still far too young to look so haggard.

Hearing the click of the door opening, as I walked in she tried to smile as she mouthed a 'Good morning'. I wanted to talk to her for I could almost feel the desperate sadness radiating from her. I asked if she would like a cup of tea as I was making one, but with a shake of her head she got up from her chair and within seconds had left the room. It seemed that she didn't even have the will left to talk as the others had.

I really felt that being open about what had happened helped me see more clearly the mistakes I had made, ones that had placed my feet firmly on the path leading to the refuge. Not only that, but I was determined that it was time to map out my future and decide what it was I wanted to do. For it was not just my future I had to think of, but my children's as well. Not that I talked about my future too much. I understood that the plans fermenting in my head would not be as easy for the others to achieve. Although we ate our meals together, we had to accept that our friendship was only a temporary one: we all knew that we would not meet again once we were in the outside world.

'Soon,' Farah told me one evening, 'there will be a call to the refuge saying a place has been found for one of us. A car will turn up and take us there. We will just disappear into another life until we are convinced that no one is relentlessly looking for us.'

I felt a lump form in my throat when I thought of the loneliness these women would be walking into. Their culture was one where few women would have been living on their own. I felt then that I was lucky – it would not be that long before I would have a safe place for myself and my children. So, soon, I would be able to have a life again. Unlike the other women, I only had one man to be scared of and I was pretty sure that Dave would give up looking for me. And if I saw him anywhere near me, a quick call to the police would sort that out.

I learnt a little later that the huge problem that the other women had was that they might not recognise some of the men who were searching for them – they could be distant cousins or uncles that they had never met.

It was an evening when one of our conversations sprang up that explained that fully to me. I had just put Justin to bed and fed Jade, then checked that the baby monitor was on and came back into the community room. The scene that greeted me was of all the women brushing each other's hair.

'This is something we like doing for each other when we are together,' one of them told me. 'We only have to cover it when we go outside or if there are males in the house. Not that we are usually allowed to meet them so I suppose in our culture we need the company of other women even more than yours does.'

'Yes, women have to look out for each other all right,' Farah said. 'If we don't, then who will? Still, not having our faces seen by men outside our family should make us safer. Means there aren't many people who would recognise us when we leave here.'

And I began to understand then that it was not only their husbands finding them that they were afraid of.

'There are also not many photos of us uncovered that could be passed around to relatives and we would hardly be recognised from the few that have been taken,' Amira said.

'I've thought of that,' Farah said rather solemnly. 'Because that's something that has bothered me. Both my mother and I were wearing Western dress when I first met my husband. My father took a lot of photos of us then, my husband and I had copies of all of them. And of course there were my wedding ones as well. With my hair, I really stand out though I suppose

I could dye it. I don't know if my husband kept those photos – I should have looked for them when I was leaving, but I didn't have time.'

I had recognised something in the cadence in her voice the first time I had heard her speak, but didn't like to ask any questions as to where she came from. Now I thought Farah wouldn't object to me asking a simple question: 'It's Iran you come from, isn't it?' I asked. 'I sort of picked up on your accent because there were some girls at my school from there that I was friendly with.'

'Yes,' she answered, smiling. 'From what I've heard, it was once a wonderful country. My parents left when I was no more than a baby so any memories of it aren't mine, they are my mother's. She used to tell me stories of what it was like when she was young as she pulled out photos for me to see from a box of her most treasured ones. She gave me a lot of them so I would see how the country had once been. She wanted me to understand her early life in a place she saw as beautiful. Which it was, until everything changed, that is.

'When she was my age, her life was so different. Women wore Western clothes and make-up when they went out. They could meet friends of both sexes in the coffee shops and choose who it was they wanted to marry. But then everything changed,' Farah said sadly.

'What happened?' I asked for my knowledge of Iranian history was not great.

But she didn't answer straight away, her face turned from me and I saw that what was left of her spirit had travelled in time to the place her family once saw as home.

'Our ruler the Shah was forced to leave the country in 1979. He went into exile. The monarchy was abolished and the country came under strict Islamic rule. Which meant the old rules were enforced. That was goodbye to freedom for all the women. Can you imagine what it would be like for your politicians to tell you what to wear, where you could go and then forbid you painting your nails or putting make-up on your face? Because that's what happened almost overnight. My parents decided to leave the country – they didn't want their children to grow up there, especially as my mother had given birth to a daughter. They managed to come to England because there were many other Iranians who had left when they did, for they too didn't want their wives and daughters to lose their freedom.'

'So, your parents came here to escape that regime?'

'They did. My father set up a small restaurant serving Middle Eastern food and when that became popular, they opened a deli as well. And both businesses did really well.'

'I suppose you haven't managed to bring any of those photos you mentioned with you here?'

She looked tearful at this question and then explained that her husband had ripped every one of them into tiny pieces.

'Why? I mean, it's your family, that was a dreadful thing to do!'

'My husband believed in all of Iran's new rules. "Your parents disobeyed the rules," he would tell me. He was really angry when he saw me looking at the photos. "They'll have to obey them now," he added gloatingly.

'My parents loved it over here, but they missed their families and their own parents. The last time they visited made them worry as they had grown older and frailer, and both of them felt it was their duty to return to Iran, even though they would have to obey the strict laws there. Though they got letters coming from different members of the family that kept telling them it was not so bad and that they managed to still have a good life.

'Over the years since they left, they had taken holidays in Iran and they took me with them once. It was nice meeting all my family, but that didn't make it a place that I would ever want to live in, but then I grew up here, not there. They had a reasonable amount of money put away as well. A lump sum was placed in my bank account when I turned twenty-one. Not that it's there anymore.'

'So they left England and went back?'

'Yes, but not straight away. I also have two brothers in another part of the UK and plenty of friends where we lived, although that didn't stop them being concerned about leaving me. It was at one of their friends' dinner parties that I met the man who became my husband. I thought the pair of us had clicked almost straight away, I didn't think for one moment that he made sure of that. He asked me out that evening and after I had been seeing him for a while, my parents were delighted that I had found someone who they believed was really nice and came from a similar background to myself.

'I thought he was ideal as well. He made me feel that we had a lot in common. Same interests, he took me to the theatre and we talked about books. He was so polite and considerate, I could hardly believe I had found someone like him. Can't believe it now either. Neither my parents nor myself had any idea that he believed in the old rules which meant women, in his opinion, had limited uses apart from cooking, cleaning and bearing their husband sons.

'He knew my parents were very well off, of course. Not that he ever mentioned it. They had not left Iran without money and on top of that, their businesses had expanded. It took me a while to realise it was knowing that which had spurred him on to court me. I never found out how he knew about the money in my account, but he did.

'So, right up until my parents caught that plane back to Iran, no one knew the man he really was. Well, apart from his two brothers, I suppose, who acted the same as my husband. And his mother doted on him as he was her youngest son. I thought she was a crotchety old woman but we just put that down to her age. She didn't come to our wedding, but excuses were made of her not being well enough. Of course, she did not want to be around women, especially Iranian women, who would be dressed in the way she despised.'

'What did he do for a living?' Amira asked.

'Good question, that. Once I was married, I was not that sure. When he met me, he was working in an accountancy firm. I remember my father saying he had a decent job.'

I stopped myself from asking if she did not have other relatives that could have helped her as I suddenly remembered the caution of not asking questions.

'It hardly took more than a day or two once my parents left for him to begin to show his true self. He moved his mother in with us. She was a horrible old harridan who hated me. She would glare at me before and was now more disapproving every day. He thought she was wonderful and wanted me to produce three sons as she had.

'"Now that's something a woman can be proud of," he told me. But no matter how many times he lay on top of me grunting like an animal, I never got pregnant.

'As the months passed and there was no sign that I had conceived, he really changed. Or at least I suppose he just showed me the man he really was. He told me I had not been honest with him, that I must have known there was something wrong with me and so must my "bloody Western-dressed mother".

'Another accusation he came out with was that being such a Western girl, I must have slept with so many men that my insides were damaged. And that's when the beatings began. He had already stopped me working. Straight away, he insisted that when I left the house I must wear the burka. Which made me feel, when we went out, that fingers were pointing at me. No one, it seemed, was interested in who the person underneath it was; I sometimes felt I was invisible. And there were his brothers and my husband strutting around in their leather jackets and smart jeans. Girls stared at them, but I think they felt pity for three such handsome men having a woman like me walking behind them.'

I wanted to ask what happened next as she stopped talking and poured out some of what she called her 'calming tea' and passed the cups around. I was wondering how she had escaped that house and she, guessing that's what we all wanted to know, took a deep breath as she finished her story: 'The beatings were bad enough, but when my periods came he made me sleep in that tiny little place just outside the kitchen, the one where the washing machine was. He had put a small mattress in there and each night, I placed it on the floor and slept under the only blanket he would allow for my bedding. That was because, he told me, period time makes a woman dirty and he only wanted me in the bedroom for sex. It was quite a relief when he said that he no longer wanted me to stay in the room and after he had his orgasm, I was to go downstairs and sleep on the mattress.

'In case you are wondering, Ava, why I did not run from that house, I couldn't. All the doors were locked. The keys were in the old witch's bag. Short of knocking her out, which I often felt like doing, there was no way I could leave. I had no money either and no ID – he had taken my passport and driving licence as well as all my bank cards. I had no reason for needing any of them, he told me. Maybe if the violence had begun earlier, I might have had the gumption to do just that, but by then, I was too cowering. It was when his violence grew worse that some of my courage returned.'

She paused and rolled up her sleeve to show a large patch of pink, puckered skin. 'That's what he did two days before I managed to escape and that is when I realised that bad as my life was, it was only going to get worse. The one thing my husband did not accept was that I'm knowledgeable about computers and his was easy to get into. It was when he was out that I googled an organisation that would help me and scribbled down the number. His mother used to have a nap in the afternoon. I had noticed that as she was getting older, she was also becoming more forgetful. Which was a real stroke of luck, because she had left her bag downstairs.

'That's when I made the call. I was so scared she would hear me that I was shaking with fear. That's also why I didn't dare go into the room where my belongings were – I didn't want her to hear my feet going up the creaking stairs. There was a downstairs lavatory, which I was told to use when she was resting.

'A driver was sent to collect me – "Just go out of the door and turn left. Someone will be there in ten minutes." I was shaking with terror, I can't tell you how scared I was. No money, no clothes, but she had a jar, where my husband placed money in case his mother needed to go shopping.'

'You didn't!'

'I did! There was only about twenty pounds or so in it and I tipped it into a plastic bag, praying the coins wouldn't clink. I went out of the back door because she would have heard the front one close and walked as calmly as I could to where the driver would be.

'It was a woman who came for me, the person on the phone had told me that it was a women-only taxi company, who they had used more than once. And when she opened the car door to let me in, I could have cried with the relief at getting away from that house and everyone in it.'

8

It was Denise who finally got Fareeda to talk after she had surprised us all by asking if it was all right to join us in the lounge. Of course, we told her yes, and judging by the smiles, everyone was really pleased that she wanted to do so. Until then, as far as we were concerned, Denise was just one of the women who looked after us. That evening, we had no idea that she too had a story to tell: she had decided that the time was right to share it with us.

Tea was poured out for her and then we started to ask her questions about the refuge. I said she must have seen so many people come and go.

'I have, and most of them leave here to go on to a better life,' Denise said and then began to tell us a little about the refuge's history. 'The first one was opened way back in the seventies,' she said. 'Now that might seem a long time ago because you four weren't even born then, but in actual fact, for a lot of abused women, it seems like yesterday. It was largely due to a wonderful woman called Erin Pizzey and all those who supported her that the laws were changed to do more to protect women. Back then, if a man raped his wife, even his estranged one, it was not illegal. If a woman was beaten by her husband and sought help from either the police or her church, she was just told to go back to him. That generation of police did not want to interfere in what they called "a bit of a domestic". They only got involved if every bone in the woman's body was broken and she was fighting for her life in intensive care. OK, it was not quite so bad as that,' she added quickly when she saw the dismayed expressions on the women's faces, 'but it was bad enough. Right up to the seventies and even later, married women who had been battered were expected to do their best to be a better wife and make it up with their husbands. Many felt they were to blame for arousing their spouses' anger and tried to hide their black eyes and bruises from friends and neighbours.'

'That's so true,' I said. 'Scarves became my accessories, as did sunglasses when even thickly applied make-up couldn't hide those black eyes. I tried the lot. And I did feel shame! I didn't want my friends to know what was happening, so I kept making excuses not to see them.'

'Exactly, Ava, that is how most of us react. That shame women have been made to feel is like a dead weight on their shoulders. It was the opening of refuges that began to change lives. The first one was back in the seventies. It didn't take long for women to hear that there was a place of safety that welcomed them and that gave them both hope and courage. The phone number was passed around and within days, every room was occupied with battered and frightened women and their fearful small children. It was realising that they were not the only ones who had lived with a violent husband that helped them get their strength back. When they had recovered sufficiently and heard that other houses were being turned into places of safety, many of them volunteered to work in them. In fact, I've met one of the very first women to walk through the London refuge's door. She told me no sooner had the front door opened than a pair of arms went round her and she heard words that she never thought she would: "Welcome, you are safe now." She worked at the refuge for some time, wanting to give back what she had received: kindness and compassion. And over the years since they first opened, many have followed her.

'Why am I telling you all this, you might ask? Because I too am one of those women. Well, not one of the ones from the seventies,' she said, grinning slightly and we all chuckled a bit. 'However, I was in a refuge with my two children just over twelve years ago. I heard what you said, Farah, about your husband obeying the old rules. Well, believe me there are a great deal of men born in our country who do so as well. There was a time not so long ago when there were few, if any, rules to protect women in this country. And there are still men who believe it's their right to control women and punish them if they're not obedient. Those men come from all walks of life. There have been wives of rich and powerful men here and others from all different cultures and religions.'

I realised then that she wanted us to understand that we were far from being alone in having been led into relationships with violent partners. That literally thousands had been before us and most probably a great deal more would be making those phone calls long after we had left and rebuilt our lives.

'So, now you all know how I came to work here, don't you?'

Smiles came her way as heads nodded. I always thought it must take courage for her to admit she had once been a victim.

'Did you come to work here because you wanted to help other women?' Farah asked.

'Really, I want to help people to relearn how to help themselves. Make them tell themselves over and over again that they did not deserve what happened to them. No one does. Saying enough is enough and I'm leaving is something to be really proud of. All of us women should have a motto, shouldn't we?'

'Like, don't let the bastards grind you down,' I said and there were giggles and blushes all round.

'What we try and do here is to encourage you to turn your lives around,' Denise said then. 'If it hadn't been for a refuge like this, my life would never have been the same. OK, times have changed. Today's police receive training in domestic violence along with sexual violence and exploitation too.'

We waited then for her to tell us why she had gone into a refuge for it was hard to imagine this strong woman being at the mercy of an abusive man.

*   *   *

Seeing our curious faces staring expectantly at her, Denise just smiled and said, 'Anyhow, I'd better tell you what went wrong in my life. It all started when I met John, the man I married.

'You know, even though I hadn't noticed a few blips in his personality when we first met, I should at least have picked up on something strange on our wedding day. Oh, when I first met him I thought he was a charming man and he seemed to want to spend as much time with me as possible. Maybe I should have noticed that the people I met were his work colleagues, not old friends who all met up for a few drinks regularly on a Friday night. Although they were friendly, I did notice that there was not a great deal of warmth coming in his direction. I suppose I should have learnt a little more about him, but like so many women, I was happy to be with him and so I didn't ask those searching questions.'

'What sort of work did he do?' I asked.

'Not quite certain, I only knew what he had told me. Though now I'm not sure how much of it was true. The one bit I know was not a lie was that he worked for an insurance company. He told me that he was one of the top sales people there. Now I don't have a clue what he really did, but I worked out a long time ago that he was never the top salesman.

'Another clue that there was something odd about his past was when we sent our wedding invitations out. Why on earth didn't I ask a few questions then? I just don't know. Too keen on getting a ring on my finger, I suppose. Even so, I should have thought it strange that the only two people he had coming to our wedding were his parents. Neither of them appeared pleased, though they did manage to smile and say congratulations.'

'That sounds familiar,' I said. 'Dave seemed to have plenty of friends, ones he met in the pub for a few drinks, but none of them were what I'd call lifelong friends. And he never talked that much about his family either. Like you, I never questioned him about that.'

'I can remember so clearly the first time he raised his fist to me, though. I'm sure we all can – it's a memory that doesn't go away,' Denise said.

And all our heads nodded knowingly as we remembered our first time.

'It was a clenched fist right into my face. It's a wonder my nose wasn't broken, there was enough blood dripping from it. And that was just about me standing up for myself when he complained about the meal I had cooked. Of course, the first time he did what so many do, apologised profusely over and over again. And like so many women, I accepted that too and believed his excuses that he was under huge pressure at work.

'The next time though he put all the blame on me. Said I hadn't been encouraging him enough when he was working all hours to feed and clothe us. Again, I accepted that excuse and all the ones that followed until I concluded that he actually enjoyed hurting me. By the time the twins were toddling around, there was hardly a day when I didn't have bruises on my face and body.

'He gradually began getting more and more angry about just about everything. He caused scenes in shops and accused cashiers of cheating him then he'd ask why other customers were staring at him, all kinds of embarrassing things. I hated going out with him, it was getting so bad.

'It was about six months later that he began to get suspicious of me although he always had accused me of flirting or looking at other men when we were out. I remember one time, we were in a self-service restaurant – you know, the ones attached to supermarkets. There was a girl in the queue who had a mane of extraordinarily beautiful red hair. I couldn't help looking at it. He of course thought I was looking at the man who was standing behind her and that was enough for him to cause a scene right there and then. I didn't even get to eat my meal before he dragged me out by my arm.

'That was the day when my fear of him intensified because I now realised that there was something really wrong with him. And I became concerned for my twins' safety too. They were already becoming scared of him and they were barely walking. Those times when his fist rose up in the air before it descended on whichever part of me he wished to hurt were even more traumatic for them. I was so worried that their heads would not be filled with happy memories of childhood such as me reading them stories, blowing out candles on a cake and making a wish on their birthdays. Those are the childhood memories that should be locked in small children's minds, not ones of shouts and screams, a father storming out of the house and a mother with blood streaming out of her nose, trying to get herself up off the floor.

'My children didn't like going to school for the first few weeks either – they didn't like being away from me. They were scared that he would come back when they weren't there. But that didn't last long. The teachers understood what they had been through and did their best to help them.

'Eventually their father turned on them as well as me. No,

not with his fists, he had another plan. You see, he made all three of us prisoners for over a month.'

That remark caused gasps as we waited to hear the details.

'I'd better tell you how we became prisoners, seeing as you've been polite enough not to ask. Of course, it didn't happen overnight, nothing does. The first move he made was telling me to take the twins out of nursery school. It was a small one that they loved going to. I had gone back to work just part-time but I knew he wanted me to stop – I had to when he got his way, he wanted them looked after at home was what he told me. And that was the beginning of his plan to stop us leaving the flat.

'Each day, his behaviour became more erratic. I should have left him then, but I was still in the planning stage. It was not easy for me to escape my husband but I think he had worked out that I wanted to go. Any woman would have, if not for their own sake then for the safety of their children. Once he had me back at home, the beatings got worse. There was more than one occasion when he knocked me about so badly, I could hardly walk. Not that I could have walked anywhere, because during the last year we were together, he was locking us in when he left the house, which absolutely terrified me. What would happen if one of us was taken ill or there was an accident in the kitchen that started a fire were the thoughts that kept spinning around in my head. There were still a few times when we went out together with the children so that they could get fresh air. Then he always made sure there was plenty of food in the house although that all came to an end eventually. Whereas I dreaded his return, not knowing what kind of mood he might be in, I was also frightened that one day he might just leave us there.

'But for the last month all three of us became complete prisoners. He refused to let the twins and I leave the flat for any reason whatsoever. He was too busy, he told me, to take them for walks. I told him that children should not be cooped up all day and that they needed fresh air and kept asking me to take them to the park. I could tell, even if he couldn't, that they were desperate to run around a little and play with other youngsters but when I mentioned it, he just laughed at me.

'"I'm not stupid, you know," he'd say contemptuously. "I know you have plans to run off with my children and do you really think I'm going to let you do that?"

'Of course he was right, that's exactly what I would have done for I had finally reached a place where I was ready to flee. It was then that his hours became more erratic. I never knew when he would return or if he would bring us some food. Even when he did, there was never enough to go round. The twins had become paler and noticeably thinner and my own body had become quite emaciated. I still have no idea where he was on the nights he didn't return. We would all go to bed hungry but at least relieved that he had not come back, though every day and every hour, I would fear the sound of the door opening and him walking in. All too often he was fired up with alcohol, which gave him the excuse to take his temper out on me.

'By then, he wasn't bothered about where his fists would land. After all, there was no one who would notice my blackened eyes or swollen mouth. There were times I was in so much pain that I just wished I could close my eyes and slide away from this world. Perhaps if I hadn't had the children to think about, I might have done that. Throwing a hairdryer into the bathwater with me in it was a thought that kept playing through my mind, but I couldn't have left my children alone with my husband.

'The flat also seemed to grow smaller every day. It felt like the walls were closing in on me and the children couldn't understand why they couldn't go out. They were sullen and whiney, which was to be expected under the circumstances, but that didn't stop me from wanting to scream at them. Something I really had to try hard at controlling – after all, none of this was their fault.

'There was one day, not long before we managed to escape, when he knocked me out cold before he left, locking the door behind him. My poor little twins were just about hysterical when I eventually came round – they must have believed I was dead. It took me a while to calm them down as I felt so weak, I could hardly move. When I did manage to get up, my legs were really wobbly, the left side of my head was throbbing and I lurched into the bathroom to throw up in the basin.

'I became convinced that I would die in that flat. He had taken away the phone right at the beginning, so there was no one I could contact. And not only was the food he bought sparse, but there was nothing in our home which growing children need – like milk, fruit and vegetables.

'You must be wondering why the neighbours hadn't got curious or even worried about the screams from me and the sound of children crying. Trouble was the next-door flat was empty and I think the one underneath was as well. He had locked all the windows, which were double-glazed so I couldn't even put my head out to scream. Not that knowing this stopped me hammering on the walls and banging on my door.

'So, how did I escape? You must be wondering about that too.'

'We are,' we all said in hushed tones and just about in unison.

'It was complete and utter luck. For weeks I kept hoping that someone would come and look at the empty flat next door, but no one appeared. Which meant that however many times I looked through the letter box, I never saw a pair of feet. Except for a few days before I managed to escape and then they belonged to my husband.

'You can imagine how scared I was. I could just about hear the thumping of my heart as I shot away from the door as fast as I could. I knew he'd seen me and I was right, he was laughing gleefully when he came in. And then he hit me. I was too defeated to react as I felt so listless. I wanted to crawl into bed, pull a blanket over my head and block everything out, but I had the children, who still needed my attention.

'The day we got out was the one when John realised that something had gone wrong with the electricity. He grumbled that there was no light on the stairs, which could have made him fall. *I wish* was the thought that ran through my mind though as he had the keys that wouldn't have done me much good. Maybe someone would come to tell me he was dead. But what didn't enter my husband's head was if it was the electricity for the block that had failed, there was a good chance that workmen would arrive.

'I prayed that he would be out when they arrived. And guess what? My prayers were answered. After he had gone, my ear was pressed to the door and I nearly jumped with joy when I heard deep male voices outside. I called out to them through the letter box. Well, screamed actually, telling them that we were prisoners. Their feet faltered and I heard them mutter to each other something about housewives. Maybe they thought I was some neurotic woman who drank all day. What I should have done was just said that my husband had taken the keys with him and I needed to go to the shops or something like that.

'I could have cried when I heard them walk away. Surely they weren't going to ignore me? In actual fact, they went straight to their boss, who took very little time arriving at the door and calling out to me. As my words came tumbling out, he told me to take a deep breath, which I did. I explained that we had been locked in the flat for over a month, that we couldn't get any fresh air for even the windows were locked – "He's made sure there's no escape. He's taken the phone, just ripped it from the wall. And my children are getting more and more distressed," I told him.

'He asked how old they were and I was so choked up as I told him they were four-year-old twins, who didn't understand what was happening. Then he asked a couple more questions, such as how often does he come back and when?

'"Are they or you injured in any way? Do I need to phone for medical assistance?" he asked me and I told him we were all just very distressed and hungry. He didn't ask any more questions, but very calmly told me to go and sit with my children while he got one of his workmen to drill out the lock. He must have realised that my situation was really serious, perhaps even more serious than he had gleaned so far.

'Even now I can still see the look of shock on his face when that door finally opened. He saw a woman perhaps the same age as him with bruises everywhere, who could hardly stand. I saw a blond-haired man wearing jeans and a black golf shirt, looking very concerned. It must have been clear that I had lost weight too – my clothes were hanging off me. The man who had drilled the lock looked equally shocked as he stood back to allow his boss to enter.

'"I'm Gavin," the supervisor told me and then very calmly said that he would make sure the children and I got safely out of there. He only had one other question: "Did your husband do that to you?"

'The tears of shame and relief were pouring down my cheeks. I sobbed a "yes", nodding furiously.

'"We should notify the police," he said, "but only when you're ready. Are you expecting him back any time soon?"

'I explained then that I had no idea.

'"Right then, I'm making a couple of calls," he said. He explained that he was getting a mate of his to come over, who would make sure John couldn't cause any trouble. The second call would be to his wife, who had been a nurse up until their daughter was born. She would be back from taking her to school and he was going to ask her to get over here too.

'Seeing I was still shaking, he led me gently into the sitting room, where the twins were clinging to each other. I guess the male voices had scared them for they hadn't followed me. He smiled at them and said hello in such a tender way, but they just stared back at him blankly. But he didn't waste any time – one workman was sent out with a short shopping list for take-away food: burgers for breakfast with an egg on top. "And teabags and milk," I added, "oh, and juice for the boys." He then asked the man who had used the drill to keep an eye out for my husband until his mate arrived. Thankfully, John didn't show up that day.

'"Don't worry, love, he won't get anywhere near you," Gavin told me. "He'll run a mile if he sees my mate anyhow. Most probably run if he sees me too. Men like him might bully women and children, but underneath they are cowards."

'I think that his burly friend, who turned up within minutes, it seemed, was a bit disappointed that John didn't show up. When he saw my bruises and the pale, tearful faces of my two small boys, I could almost see his muscles twitch with the anticipation that he would.

'"Might not do him any harm to bump into someone my size," this giant of a man said with a chuckle. From the expression on his face I thought it might just do my husband a great deal of harm – not that I wanted to let the children see their father getting what he deserved.

'The atmosphere changed slightly when the twins saw their food being brought in. They tucked into it straight away, while mine remained untouched as I sipped at a mug of hot, sweet tea. At the same time, Gavin's wife Jill appeared.

'"Brought my first-aid kit and my camera," she told me gently.

'I heard Gavin ask if she thought I needed to go to a hospital to get checked over.

'"I don't think so, no broken bones. But I'll photograph the injuries in case this goes to court," she told him.

'It was she who told me about the refuge, a place where I would be safe until the police caught my husband. And yes, they would need to interview me in the flat. And that's what happened. I don't need to go into those details, just that they were very kind.

'It was Jill who packed up all mine and the children's clothes and drove me to the refuge. Just remembering now how kind that group of people was to us still makes me feel tearful. And when the door of the refuge opened and I walked in, for the first time in a very long while I felt safe.

'I never did go back to that flat. Although John had told me he had bought it, the truth was it was only rented. With two children, it didn't take that long for me to be rehoused. By that time John had been arrested. He never went to prison though, he was committed to a mental hospital. That's all I know about what happened to him and quite frankly, it's enough. I was granted a divorce and sole custody of the children very quickly. And can you believe it, both my boys are about to go to university! Now, Farah, is there any more chai?'

But there was silence.

'The reason I'm telling you all this is because I want you to understand that this type of abuse runs in all classes and cultures. I know it's difficult to talk about. That's because deep down, we blame ourselves. My advice? Don't.'

And saying that, she looked directly at Fareeda and smiled.

9

We all looked in Fareeda's direction too, waiting to see if she would tell us her story next. She smiled at us, then spoke softly: 'Let Amira tell you her story first, because mine is really not so unlike hers. There's another one that I have decided I want to share with you.'

'She's right, you know,' Amira told us, which made us aware that she already knew the reason why Fareeda always seemed so sad. For her sake, I hoped that she would manage to unburden herself, for I and the others had found that getting our stories out was certainly helping each one of us to come to terms with our personal trauma.

'I too was helped by the same organisation that you went to, Farah,' said Amira, who had been listening intently to every word that had been spoken. I wondered what dreadful things had happened to her, I just hated the thought that her life had been made a misery for she was such a kind and warm-hearted woman. Yet I had felt right from the first day that these women who did their best to make my life easier had been through a far worse time than me.

I waited, almost holding my breath, when Amira began her story – I kept hoping that it wasn't going to be as bad as I thought it probably was.

Amira stumbled over some of the words, but she still managed to get her story out as we all sat in silence, listening intently.

'It was my mother-in-law who helped me escape in the end,' she told us.

Which caused us all to express some surprise – wasn't her mother-in-law part of the problem?

'Oh, I assure you it wasn't because she felt sorry for me. If we had been in another country where the laws did not protect women, she wouldn't have cared less if he had killed me. But she was completely aware that as we were in the UK, the laws here had to be obeyed. She appeared to be the one member of the family who understood what trouble her sons could bring on themselves, should they ignore them.

'But my husband was an arrogant man who thought nothing of rules. I think even his brothers were worried that his brutality towards me would go too far. To him, me dying at his hands would have just been considered an honour killing in our country and almost acceptable. His excuse for beating me until I could hardly stand was because I hadn't told him I was barren. And in the UK, much to his disgust, this is not a sufficient reason for a divorce. This was what he appeared to enjoy taunting me about – how a barren wife is a useless one, one that needs replacing. No doubt he repeated that remark enough times to his family to make his mother more concerned as to what he might do to me. Call it an honour killing or whatever you like, the British laws would have called it murder, wouldn't they? And no matter what, they don't let murderers get away with it. So, I suppose I had a bit of luck in my mother-in-law telling me to go – not that she once tried to help me before.

'She was aware of those beatings he gave me, must have heard my screams fall silent when I just couldn't take the pain anymore and fainted. But she never said a word, not a hint of compassion or kindness came from her. Like him, she blamed me for not getting pregnant. She shared my husband's opinion that apart from cooking and cleaning, producing sons was all women were needed for.

'It was not long after my marriage – well, a few months or so after the ceremony – that I was treated as if I was a slave. It was she who told him each month when I was bleeding. He would glare at me then say, "I hear your womb is still empty," and apart from telling me something he wanted done, I was ignored.

'After those first few months I was no longer allowed to eat with them. After all, slaves didn't eat with their masters, did they? My mother-in-law would tell me what food I could help myself to. Not that it was ever very much, only leftovers. Just enough to keep me strong to do all the chores she had lined up for me to complete first. They wanted to see me utterly beaten down. Both of them demanded that I wait on them, hand and foot – that made my mother-in-law happy as she no longer had any cleaning or cooking to do. I had to be up early each morning, preparing their food, and by night-time, I would crawl exhausted into bed only to be raped by him.

'When they had friends round, they hardly ever saw me. I was the one in the kitchen doing all the cooking, which his mother came for and carried out. To her, I was just a servant, not a daughter-in-law and certainly not one of the family.

'The beatings were bad enough, but there came a night when he had been drinking alcohol, which he wasn't used to – it is forbidden in our culture. He went too far and that was when she decided I must leave the house.'

'So, what was the last straw that made her help you leave?' Farah asked gently.

'She accepted the beatings he gave me, she accepted him treating me like an outcast, but she could not accept this.'

And as she raised her jumper, all of us swooned in horror. The scars Farah had shown us had shocked me, but this was the worst physical abuse I had ever seen. There were cuts, deep ones, all over her back and upper arms. Some looked old, while others appeared quite fresh.

'She covered the last one with a dressing,' Amira explained. 'She was actually gentle when she did that – I suppose because she wanted me to be strong enough to leave.'

'You should have gone to a hospital, some of those cuts look really deep,' I gasped.

'They have been seen by the lovely nurse who checks us out when we arrive. I explained to you, Denise, didn't I, when I came here, why they daren't take me to hospital?'

'You did, Amira, and even I was shocked when I understood what you meant. They were right, though – there was certainly a strong chance that a hospital doctor would feel it his duty to involve the police.'

'And they would have wanted to know who had done this to me, wouldn't they?'

'So what?!' I exclaimed. 'He deserves to be arrested and banged up.'

'That's not the way the men in his family would see it. There would have been a fatwa put out on me.'

'A fatwa?'

'A death threat, one that is passed on through all the males in the families until it is decided which one would be responsible for my death. In that way the obvious suspect would also have rock-hard alibis, but Denise was able to bring in the nurse who dressed the wounds and checked them each week.'

'Here's a bit of good news though,' Denise told us. 'Have you heard of Nazir Afzal? I've seen him interviewed on TV, though I doubt if you saw that programme when you were with your mother-in-law, Amira! He's an amazing man. His family emigrated from Pakistan to the UK not long before he was born in Birmingham. He began his career as a solicitor and decided to work on the prosecuting side. Gradually he worked his way up until he became chief prosecutor and now he works with the police to bring criminals to court. He's also fought for new laws to protect women; have those who have treated them as slaves and men who have been violent towards their partners brought to court. In other words, he has become the voice for the voiceless. It's due to him that there has already been a case held in Pakistan, where the culprit who committed murder was tracked down.

'And as for suicides, he wants them investigated as well. I'm sure, Amira, your husband's mother was aware of the changes being made, which meant that how someone had died would not be easily hidden.'

'I expect you're right, Denise, and my mother-in-law was aware of that, which explains why his brothers too were scared of what might happen. Seeing that last knife wound was, as you said, Farah, the last straw. It frightened her enough into believing that the next time he attacked me could be the last before I died at his hands. I was bleeding a lot and she could tell that I was weak with all the blood loss. She did her best to fix it, dressed the wound as best she could. When she had finished, she brought me sweet warm tea for the shock and then told me that she was going to make sure her son left me alone. Which is why I think she decided to put a bed in the room next to hers for me – I could rest there until I was a little stronger, she told me. She also placed a pot in there so if I needed a pee during the night, I wouldn't have to walk to the bathroom. Though I couldn't have, as once I was in that room, she kept the door locked when she was off to bed herself or going downstairs.

'I knew then that she must be making plans for me to leave the house. It was pretty obvious that by locking the door, she was not keeping me in, but him out. Deep down, she must have known that her power over her son was limited and what he had started with me was not going to stop until he killed me.

'It took just a few days before she told me that it was time for me to leave. I was more or less able to walk, albeit a little slowly, and the worst bleeding from the wounds had stopped. She waited until my husband and his brothers were out of the house before she came and told me to get dressed – there was only her in the house so it was safe for me to go. Once I had pulled on my clothes as fast as possible, I went downstairs to where she was waiting. I had never seen her looking nervous before, but this time she certainly did.

'"I didn't dare ring for a taxi," she told me, "in case the neighbours saw it and you getting into it. But if you turn right when you leave, there's a bus stop only about a hundred yards away. The bus will take you to the station and stops there. There's one due in twenty minutes." Then she placed an old handbag on the table and showed me what was inside. I was surprised at the large bundle of notes she had put in there, alongside a mobile phone – "There's only one number in it," she explained, "and that's the one you have to ring for help. You need to get out of this town fast now. Catch the first train that's leaving, wherever it's going. My sons will be looking everywhere for you once they find out you've gone, especially as they might think that you've reported your husband to the police. For your own safety, don't even think of doing that. Just disappear and when there's no sign of you trying to cause trouble for our family, they will eventually give up looking for you. Remember to wait until you're on a train and then ring the number. It's a helpline for women who need to escape their husbands and they will help you."

'So that's what I did. Caught the bus to the station, looked at the board to see which train was leaving the soonest and bought a single ticket. But not knowing where I would get off, I bought one for the whole way. Not that I recognised any of the names of towns it also stopped at. So, when I got on that train, I had no idea where I would finally end up nor did I know which stop I should alight at.

'It was the first time I had been on a train in England and it was very different to our ones in Pakistan. I felt nervous when the train began filling up and a man sat down next to me – that was something that would never have happened in my country. I made the call, turning my head away so I couldn't be overheard – I just told the voice on the other end of the line my name. It seemed my mother-in-law had already contacted them and given a few details of why I needed help. The voice simply asked me which train I had caught; she then told me which station to get off at: "Just show your ticket," she said, "and walk outside." She then described the car which would be driven by a woman that would be taking me to a safe place.

'It was when that call finished that I could feel the tears forming – I suppose I could hardly believe that I had really escaped from the nightmare I had been living in. For the remainder of the journey I spent my time staring out of the window, looking at the places we stopped at, letting more people on and some others off. And then I finally heard them announce the name of the station I was to get off at. I had made it! That's how I ended up here with not even an overnight case, although the rescue organisation is really helpful and I was given some bits and pieces before the car even dropped me here. So you see, it was not kindness that made my mother-in-law help me escape that day, it was fear of what might happen to her family.'

10

It was after Amira had finished her story that Fareeda finally spoke. We had all felt that she was grieving and only Amira seemed to know why. I thought maybe she had lost a child but no, like the others, she too had not been able to get pregnant, she admitted sadly. But as we were to find out, she had lost someone she loved. And as her story unfolded, I could see that she was not only mourning her loss, but for the part she was still convinced she had played in it.

Fareeda looked around at us, realising we were waiting expectantly for her: 'I had better start right at the beginning,' she said with a sigh that was so resigned, we knew this was going to be difficult for her. 'It seems a long time ago, although in fact it was only a few years ago, that I was living happily in our village in Pakistan. It was not a big place and our clay brick houses were built fairly close to each other. So different from over here, where often people do not know their neighbours. Ours was a farming community, where the men were out in the fields most of the day while the women busied themselves at home. Life was a great deal easier for my generation than it had been for my grandparents. In their day the women had to walk a long way to fetch water, which they brought back to the village in huge clay pots.

'So many people seem to think that there is little education in the rural areas and certainly my husband was of that opinion. But there were schools and, luckily for our village, there was one not too many miles away. My life was peaceful, I loved everyone in my family and felt loved by them. In all the years that I spent in our village, I never knew what it would be like to feel unsafe. It was not until my monthly bleeding began that I started to feel that my life was beginning to change. I could tell that to my family I was no longer a carefree young child for I had reached an age when it was their duty to map out my future. I heard the words "suitable marriage and husband" being said quietly to each other, while glances came in my direction. This was something that for a long time I tried to push to the back of my mind until I was unable to – not that I had any clear idea of what they had in mind for me.

'I know the West really looks down on arranged marriages and in some cases they're right to do so. Good parents like mine want their daughters to be happy, but of course I have heard of some families where the parents are focused on money, and more or less sell their daughters off to someone three times their age. But then, look at the mess so many people get into when they make their own marriage choices.'

Well, we could hardly comment. I suspect Denise and I felt she had a point, we had hardly made good marriages though goodness knows what my parents might have arranged for me, I thought with horror. *Let's not go there*, I told myself and turned my attention back to Fareeda and her story ...

'It was only about three years after my first bleed when I was told that a man whose parents had lived in our village until they emigrated to the UK was coming to visit us. I was surprised to learn that he had been in correspondence with my family for some time. He was looking for a bride, one who had not been brought up in England, but had spent her childhood in the area his parents had been born in. When asked why, his reply was that he had no wish to marry a woman who had gone to school and maybe even college in the UK, where she would have mixed with children and teenagers with Western ways – "Too many girls from our culture," he said, "have forgotten their religion and adopted the Western way of life." Which was why he wanted to find a suitable bride from "the old country", as he called Pakistan. That was the reason, I realised, why he had travelled all the way to where we lived – and it was me he wanted to meet.

'Of course my family were nervous about him coming to visit us – from the letters they had received, they saw him as a cultured businessman who had done very well for himself. He would be used to city life, where they had theatres and smart restaurants which doubtless he would eat in. Here, after it had been arranged that my two brothers would stay with their grandparents, he would still only have a small room to sleep in and his meals would be cooked by both my mother and me. Not that my family had any conceivable reason not to feel relaxed when he arrived. He just about admired everything and told us it was so wonderful to be in the village where his parents had grown up. He even said that in his mind he could see their younger selves seated with our family, eating all the local dishes his mother still cooked.

'I came to realise that his family and mine had been corresponding before I had even turned twelve. Oh, in case you're wondering why they chose my family to write to, I guess it was his mother's idea. Evidently his father had died several years before I met my husband but I was unaware of his existence almost right up to the time his letter arrived, saying he had booked the ticket for his visit.

'I was a fairly young girl when I first saw him. He was sleekly dressed in a way that only men who live in the cities are. There was a large gold watch on his arm and I noticed then that his shirt cuffs were pristine and white – I imagined that he must have bought a clean one on his way to the village for I didn't see a single crease in it. Oh, he was charming all right – there were little gifts for my family and beautiful fine wool shawls for both my mother and me. I just didn't feel a scrap of warmth coming from him as his eyes went up and down my body. Although I tried, I didn't feel particularly at ease with him – I felt that instead of trying to get to know me, he was just assessing whether I was a good choice.

'Still, my parents seemed delighted with him and believed that even though he was a lot older than me, he would make a good husband. Over our evening meal he asked me who had done the cooking in English, a question I was able to answer quite fluently in my best English. For the first time, a warm smile came in my direction. It was then that I realised that my English lessons had been his idea and he must have paid for them. Which I suppose made me grateful, for the thought of being taken to a country where I could not speak one word of the language would have been frightening. But he didn't want the future mother of his children embarrassing him – I might be a village girl, but he didn't want to appear unsophisticated.

'Now there's little to tell about what happened to me after that – just that I married him and was brought to England. All I can say is that underneath the charm that had fooled my family was a cruel, selfish man, who only wanted a woman who would obey his every command and produce the children he expected her to. And when no baby arrived? I'll leave it to you to think of what my life was like then.

'My escape was not so different from Amira's, only I used my mother-in-law's lack of English to take a risk when I accompanied her to do some shopping. I had written a note saying what was happening to me and I had to escape. I asked the shopkeeper if she could show me where a particular spice was and as we walked over to it, I slipped the note to her. Then she said she had to wait for a delivery for one thing on my shopping list – "Oh, your favourite coffee isn't here until tomorrow or the next day," she said loudly as she walked me back to the till. I quickly translated that to my mother-in-law, who muttered away.

'When we went back to the shop three days later to collect the coffee and a couple more items, the shopkeeper quickly placed them in my bag. Only this time there was more than just our shopping in it: underneath was a note from her. It told me that a car would be waiting outside the front door and the driver would take me to a safe place. She gave the time, which was early afternoon, when, as I had put in my note, my mother-in-law would be taking her afternoon nap.

'Luckily, the old witch didn't bother to lock the doors and I suppose she never thought that I might run away – after all, I was married to her wonderful son and besides, I had no money at all. In the whole time of my marriage I was never even given one pound.'

'So did you just walk out?' I asked.

'Yes, and as promised, there was the car with a woman sitting in the driver's seat. As soon as she saw me, the back door swung open and I hopped in and lay down on the back seat so I couldn't be seen. My mother-in-law must have heard the front door open and rushed out of her room to see what was happening. The driver, who quickly introduced herself as June as she roared off, told me with a bit of a laugh that she had seen an old woman in her rear-view mirror, standing in the doorway of the house with her head turning left to right and back again.

'"She must have thought you disappeared into thin air," June said with a chuckle. "Good that, I hardly wanted to strong-arm someone her age." I'm still not sure if she was joking.

'That's all I need to tell you about me.'

11

There was silence as we waited patiently for Fareeda to tell us the part of her story that had caused her so much grief. I think we all felt that this one was not going to have a happy ending. It only took her first sentence to make us hold our breath.

'Once I had a little sister, who my parents named Ayanna. All our names have a meaning and hers meant "innocent beautiful flower" – a name that could not have described her any better – whereas my name, Fareeda, means unique.

'I can remember so well the night my mother gave birth to Ayanna. I was waiting to find out if I was going to have a baby sister or another brother and so hoping for the first. I could not bring myself to go to bed, nor did my father tell me to. He just smiled at me and muttered that it might be a long night. Ayanna was, I decided, the most beautiful baby I had ever seen. I simply loved her right from that first moment.

'By the time she reached five, the fine, black hair which had been on her baby head had grown long and glossy, and I braided it every day. Those braids of hers, flying behind her when she ran out of the house to play, made me smile, for her happiness was also my happiness. She was not just an extraordinarily pretty child, but one with an equally beautiful nature. A joyous little creature who all the villagers simply doted on and repeatedly said so too. When I left home she was still a child in my eyes, though old enough for me to see how exquisite a woman she was going to be. Young as she was, I noticed how the boys could hardly take their eyes off her. I'm sure that there were quite a few of them who begged their parents to ask if they could marry her.

'When I left to go to the UK with my husband, it nearly broke my heart to say goodbye to her. Not that I had any choice, for my husband was a man who had charmed my parents from the first day he had arrived. They told me I was so lucky to have a man like him asking for their permission to marry me; they believed that my life was really going to be a happy and comfortable one. On the day of our departure the whole village came out to say goodbye. A little earlier I had managed to have just a few minutes alone with Ayanna – she was only nine then – and I felt such a tug at my heart when I noticed the tears in her huge brown eyes that were threatening to spill down her cheeks. She said she could hardly bear the thought of not seeing me again for a long time, she just hugged and hugged me and made me promise to write to her every week.

'A promise I have regretted making for a very long time.

'What I didn't guess then was that it would not be that many years before she was back in my life. Once my brother-in-law had seen the photos my husband had taken in the village, he too had begun corresponding with my family.

As soon as he saw her photo, he had decided my sister was the girl he wished to marry.

'Like my husband, he was a great deal older than her, but clearly wealthy. And I fear my letters had confirmed that view. Did my descriptions of my life lead my parents to believe that she too was going to marry a man who would spoil her? I was trying not to worry them by not revealing my unhappiness, so I represented my life in more glowing terms.

'When I heard about the wedding, I was truly horrified. I wanted to scream with despair but I could not stop her marrying into this family. The men in it were, I believed, totally incapable of looking after anyone but themselves and I suppose their mothers. If only I could have warned my parents, but I had no way of doing that. Maybe my husband had thought I was crafty enough to find a way of sending a letter, for I knew nothing until the wedding day was imminent.'

'Didn't she have any say in who she married?' I asked.

'Only a little, but knowing my family, they would have thought that despite the age gap he would make a good husband. After all, I was part of that family and appeared to be happy, for didn't my letters say so? Though maybe if she had really protested, I think, with her being their much-loved youngest child, they would have accepted her wishes. She really was, as you say over here, the apple of my mother's eye.

'He would paint glowing pictures of how wonderful life in England was. And she, believing every word he uttered, dreamt of the life she would have once she arrived there. Not that it was a life she was going to have for long.

'He certainly managed to convince the whole family that

England must be a wonderful country, a place where girls married to men like him lived in luxury and were treated like princesses. And I ask myself every day would my little sister have believed that if I had not written all those letters? I keep telling myself that I was not to know why I was made to do so. But I do now. My husband and his brothers shared a dream, one where they wanted docile wives who would bear them sons; sons who they could train to become part of their growing business. Their plan for the future was to build an empire which over the years would become a family dynasty. And if daughters came along, well then, they would be made to marry the right husbands who would also be an asset to their business.

'I'm sure you will all understand why I'm haunted by my guilt over writing those letters – I can't get the thought out of my head that it was because of me that my family believed he was offering their daughter a wonderful future. There's hardly a minute that goes by when I don't think of those pages of lies that were posted to my family. Those lies convinced them that I was leading a good life and that made them happy. I just wish somehow I might have found a way of sending them other letters telling the truth, not what my husband dictated to me, but I had no money, not even enough to buy my own stamps, and even if I had, the few times I left the house I was never on my own.

'Nearly every sentence I wrote described something different from the life we had in the village. A film I hadn't watched in a cinema, a restaurant I hadn't eaten in, clothes I was never able to wear and afternoon tea with friends I did not have. I know it was the thought of sharing that life with me, her older sister, that excited Ayanna. And the biggest lie of all was that my husband was sympathetic about how I felt sad at still not having a baby to hold in my arms. I hadn't been able to write about his anger at that, the hours I spent scrubbing and cleaning; how I did more daily work than any of the women in our village had to. That would have put them off. It was a huge house and I was expected to clean it on a daily basis.

'I nearly cried when I received the last letter my sister had written to me, which was all about the wedding and telling me how she could hardly wait to see me again. They would settle in a house in London that he had bought for them. One with plenty of bedrooms, which he wanted filled with children. I saw from the description that it was not far from where we lived. Something else I did not know anything about.

'At the end of her letter she wrote how much she was looking forward to spending time with me. And when she had told her husband that, he said of course she would be able to. She really believed that she and I would be able to spend days together, doing all the things she had seen well-dressed women doing in magazines: wearing our pretty outfits as we had afternoon tea in smart hotels, meeting all my glamorous friends and going shopping together. None of that was ever going to happen, was it? I had no friends, no wonderful outfits and any shopping I did was for groceries with my one and only companion, my old, bad-tempered mother-in-law.

'I thought of Ayanna being greeted by the stewardess as she stepped onto the plane and was shown to her seat. No doubt he had booked them in either business or first class, which after the hotel they had stayed in for a couple of nights would have been another sign of all the luxury to come. I wondered how she would feel when hours later, the plane landed at the time of year when the sky was grey and chilling winds nipped both ankles and faces. Not only was it wet and cold for months on end but without our family nearby, I thought that like me, she would feel lonely. I could only hope and pray that she would be given a different life to the one I had. That she would become pregnant quickly, which would please his family, especially if her firstborn was a boy. For that, she would be well rewarded. Not that I believed my brother-in-law had any kindness in him, but at least it might make him content.

'I kept wishing I could turn back the clock and refuse to write those letters even though not obeying my husband and his family would cause me more physical pain than I could have handled. But had I known what the outcome would be, I would have willingly sacrificed my life.

'Naturally, my husband invited them both over for dinner. I was told to dress nicely.

'"And wear that jewellery I gave you," he said without a trace of a smile. "You know, the pieces I bought when I believed I had married the right wife."

'So, I knew this was to be a charade, where in front of my sister and her husband we were going to pretend everything was fine between us. Of course what I really wished for was to spend a whole day alone with her, something my husband had made clear was unlikely ever to happen. Maybe he had an inkling even then that my sister might not be happy in her marriage and I might just tell her the truth about mine. The last thing they would want was us plotting anything together, such as escaping from them.

'Almost from the first moment I saw her, all smiles as she came through the door and threw her arms around me, we both exclaimed how much we had been looking forward to seeing each other.

'"Let me look at you," I said, holding her at arm's length so I could see her more clearly. "You were still a little girl when I left!"

'"I have to thank my husband for that," was her reply and I can remember how quickly she made that remark and how she included him in her winning smile. Standing only inches away from her, I felt dismay as I caught the lascivious glint in the depths of his eyes that he did not even try and hide the whole evening. He, with his increasing girth and thinning hair already turning grey, already looked like a lecherous man entering middle age. She, on the other hand, looked more like a bewildered child.

'It dawned on me that my sister was no more than a pretty little doll to him. One he owned and could do whatever he liked with. I felt sick when I saw his hands touching her body at every opportunity: it was not answering desire that I saw in her eyes when his hand stroked her, it was fear.'

* * *

'So what was the rest of the evening like?' Denise asked.

'I could say that on the surface, it was pleasant. Ayanna managed to sit close to me once the meal was over and we had moved into the living room. She made sure she smiled in her husband's direction when she chattered about anything she had done with him. She told me how thrilling it was to be taken into the kind of shops she had never been in before. She showed me the leather handbag he had bought her and then pointed to her matching shoes. Yes, they were pretty, but the sister I had known had more interests than just clothes. To me, it felt as if she was playing a part. It was that which made me feel that her chatter and the constant smiles directed towards her husband were done to cover something up, though whatever it was, she still managed to keep the smile set on her face as she told me about the beautiful home they were moving into – "Plenty of bedrooms, which we both want filled," she announced with another warm, intimate beam directed at her husband. And he, hearing her remarks, reciprocated the gesture before turning to my husband and inviting us both over to view their new house.

She might have fooled everyone else in the room, but not me. I was only too aware of how she managed to catch his eye each time she said something flattering about him. It hadn't taken me long to realise that nearly every word she uttered was to please him and not anyone else. I just wished I could have spent some time with her alone and then I could have found out how she really felt. For however bright she managed to be, it didn't stop me feeling extremely worried about her.

'The whole evening, I felt that no matter how much she mentioned all the wonderful places she been taken to, she was covering up a great deal, but then she could hardly tell me anything in the middle of a dinner party, could she? It was when I went to get us all coffee and she offered to help and followed me there that she told me her husband acted as though he was proud of her and that the men he knew looked pretty impressed, although she wasn't too sure that the women were – "Maybe it's because I still look very young," she said with a shrug. And I told her laughingly that she was most probably right there – I mean, what else could I say?

'We didn't stay in the kitchen any longer than was necessary. "Better take it in quickly," she warned as she put cups and a milk jug onto the tray because she didn't want her husband to think we were talking about him. That was the only negative thing she had said about him throughout that evening, but still those few words told me a lot and certainly did not make me worry any less.

'When the evening came to an end and our invitation to visit was repeated, I remember my brother-in-law saying that his wife had been taught to cook well as he gave her a pat on the behind, which I could tell really embarrassed her: men do not touch women in public where we come from. It was a week later when, hardly saying a word to me, my husband drove us over to his brother's house.

'"We too would have had a house like this if you had managed to do what I married you for," my husband said.

'I no longer felt angry at those comments, just numb. Didn't he think for one moment that I would also have liked a child? He had never shown an ounce of sympathy when I had gone for tests nor questioned me about the results. Not that I would have dared tell him that the female gynaecologist I consulted had told me there was no reason why I could not get pregnant. It was she who suggested my husband also needed to be tested. Much to my relief, my sister's arrival meant he left me alone. Not only had the beatings stopped but he no longer wanted me in his bed. Most probably his brother had said he didn't want Ayanna seeing bruises and getting frightened: he wanted her calm and pregnant.

'Standing inside, waiting to greet us was my sister who, dressed in a pink silk sari, her thick hair caught up in a glossy chignon, looked every inch the wife of a prosperous man. Or, as the English might say, a glamorous trophy wife. This time there were no girlish hugs, just a wide smile. She told me later that he had complained of her wrapping her arms around me because it was "too childish".

'"Ayanna can show you around," he told me once we were inside. "Got some business to talk about with my brother."

'It was in their bedroom that she told me very quietly that she did not like what he called "lovemaking". Before I could ask her anything, she just whispered that she did her best to pretend to – "Not that he really cares, as long as he's satisfied," was her last remark before she quickly ushered me out of the room. I could see then that she was nervous. He, no doubt, wanted everything we had said to each other repeated to him. I could just see him firing questions at her, but then my little sister was far smarter than he knew – she would not be easy to trip up.

'In fact, it took her a long time before she was able to confide in me more. To begin with, the two men hardly ever let us be together on our own but gradually, as our conversation seemed to bore them, they relaxed. No doubt when we disappeared into the kitchen or garden, they thought that we were only talking about women's thing – swapping recipes, that kind of thing. They would have been wrong there, because that's when she finally told me what he was like in the bedroom.

'"There is no love in what he does to me, but then he doesn't love me. He just wants to get me pregnant and he's getting impatient because it hasn't happened yet. Nothing stops him trying every single night. He keeps saying he's try-ing to make a baby and I should want him to. It's just he's so much heavier than me – I'm always scared he'll squash me flat. I hate it anyhow, the feel of his flabby stomach when he bounces up and down on me. I'm almost pleased when I have my monthly bleed, though it scares me as well, because it makes him so very angry. But at least it stops him getting on top of me. Though there are other things he makes me do then. Horrible things ..."

'I cringed at the thought of what they might be.

'"When he's in a good mood, he tells me my life will be re-ally comfortable if I produce a son for him. I'll have a nanny to help and I needn't worry about anything else except mak-ing myself pretty. But having a nanny in to look after my baby is the last thing I need – I'm bored being alone every day. He already has a gardener who I am not allowed to talk to, he forbids me to go outside when he is working. And there is a cleaner who he must have told not to talk too much, for she seems scared to stop working and avoids me. I've asked him if I could come and visit you, but he just says not yet, or tells me to wait until he's ready to invite you both over. Anyhow, he says you never go out. And you don't, do you? I know your husband's not been buying you lots of clothes. You wear the same ones nearly every time I see you. And I can tell that you're not happy – you might smile, but there is sadness in your eyes."

'There was no point in lying to her. Neither of us was happy in our marriages. But all I said on that occasion was that he was not the man I had thought he would be when I agreed to marry him. And then she asked the question I had been waiting for: "Those letters you sent us were not true, were they?"

'"No," I answered.

'"They made you write them, didn't they?"

'"Yes."

'"He's cruel to you, isn't he?"

'"I don't want to talk about that, let's talk about you instead."

'"My life is not the one I pretend to have any more than yours has been. He keeps telling me I'd better get pregnant soon or my life won't be so easy. Not that I can think what would make it worse."

'It was not long after that conversation that the brothers stopped meeting, which meant I was unable to see my sister at all. I overheard my husband telling his mother that it was because he had teased his brother about the fact there was still no baby in that big house yet. A glare came in my direction from both of them then.

'"Barren women must run in that family," his mother said with a sneer.

'It was summer when I was able to meet up with my sister

again. I knew she had not managed to get pregnant as I would have heard if she had and I was scared about the treatment an angry brother-in-law would be inflicting on her.

'Once they arrived, I was shocked to see the change in her. Not only was she thinner but all her youthful radiance had disappeared; she looked utterly defeated. She no longer managed to send her husband those bright intimate smiles, not that he would have wanted to see them. It was clear that the brothers had made up whatever row they had had.

'This time she did not try and cover up what her life was like. And listening to her, I worked out just how bad their bedroom life was. For it was in there that he punished her not by beatings but by sexual acts that were even worse. She was so tiny, almost certainly weighing not much more than seven stone, and he would have been more than double that. And in that house, she was completely powerless. He never had been affectionate, not even on their honeymoon – he just wanted to thrust himself into her. Squeeze parts of her body until they were sore: her bottom, her delicate small breasts. She said that he also sank his teeth into her, drawing blood from her nipples. Right from the beginning of their marriage, he had worked out the dates when she would be at her most fertile. He placed pillows under her until her lower half was higher and then he would push and push himself into her.

'And then she told me almost in a whisper that when her monthly bleed arrived, he did something so horrible to her that she was ashamed to tell me: he turned her over, slid a pillow under her stomach and then penetrated her until she bled from there.

'I felt a wave of nausea at the thought of what this man had done and would do again to my sister.

'"I was sore for days that first time," she told me. "Even walking was difficult and he only laughed at me then."

'Once she had managed to sweep aside the barriers of her shame she was able to tell me a lot more. And every word she uttered made me shake with rage. I don't know what part of his depravity was worse. And then there was that other thing he wanted her to do: to lean over him while he squeezed her breasts hard and take that repulsive thing between his leg and put it in her mouth.

'The first time she had closed her mouth too firmly but he was not having that. He straddled her, pushed her lips open as he told her menacingly that if her teeth touched it, she would be lucky to have any left by the morning.

'You can imagine how many times I cried at the thought of what those letters I had written had led to. From what she told me, his acts were more or less rape. She was his and he could do what he liked; every perverse desire he had was performed on her. I can't bring myself to describe them all to you, but there were more.

'She asked me if there was a way we could escape together – she could not face being with him any longer. Surely the fact I spoke English would help us? That's when I whispered that I could only go out with my mother-in-law and if I tried to run off, she would phone her sons and they would find me before I got very far. And the only English people I met were the ones who worked in shops.

'I tried to think what I could do to rescue my baby sister.

If only I had known then that there was help for women like us, but I had no idea that there were helplines and refuges. Nor did I realise that if we lived in England then we came under the protection of British law.

'I thought about what I had said, about the only English people I met being the ones in the shops. There was one shop where the owner was always friendly; in the end, she was the one I told you about, the one who helped me. I made sure to let her see the bruises on my face and then I saw her expression. She whispered a question when I was looking for something on the shelves: did I need help? And I just nodded.

'What I can never forgive myself for was that I managed to escape, but not in time to help my sister. The last time I saw her, I said I had a plan – which in the end was the one that I used. But it was too late to take her with me – suddenly, with no reason given, I was unable to see her. My brother-in-law still came to the house, but never with her. Perhaps that shrewd old witch of a mother-in-law's instinct told her that we were planning something – I don't know and I never will now.

'I only asked her once why Ayanna didn't come any more and if she was ill. She just cast a scornful look in my direction and told me they had decided it was for the best.

'The mistake my brother-in-law made was that he did not lock her inside that big bleak house where she was left alone for hours on end. The fact that she did not speak English made her a prisoner, he thought. And the phone was locked so she could not make any calls to me or our family. But he was wrong there: she spoke some English. During the time when he wanted to show her around the area she had memorised the streets, knew where the railway tracks were and which ones ran under a bridge. She felt there was only one way to escape him and she diligently planned every one of her actions.

'Now that the cleaner no longer came, she could not ask her for help. Nor could she ask the gardener, who had cast her a few friendly smiles when he saw her looking out through the window, for he only came when her husband was there. The really sad thing was that there were neighbours who would have helped her but they were English and she was so beaten down that it never entered her head to ask them.

'Which meant that escaping from her husband was something she had to do alone.

'Not only was she determined to leave him, she also wanted revenge so that once she was gone, there would be questions asked and gossip created. She knew enough about the people she had grown up with to know how rumours can travel as fast as the speed of light; she wanted to turn the community her husband and his brothers were part of against them. Ayanna might not have wished to stay in this world, but she did not want to leave a happy, blameless husband behind so she wrote down every single reason for what she had planned to do on several pages. She then placed these pages in an envelope and wrote "Pakistani Embassy, London" on it. And that was all – nothing to any of her family, not even me. But then what could she have put in writing that would have made us feel better? Nothing.

'Once she was ready, she left the house for the last time. The only thing she took with her was a handbag containing her passport and the letter. She wanted her identity to be known.

'So, my beautiful graceful sister walked the streets with only one thought in her head. Many people saw her, I know that too.

'The other image that will never leave me is what happened when she reached the bridge which the trains run under. She leant on it, waiting until she heard one coming and then with her hands pressed onto the wall, she pulled herself up on it and stood there, poised.

'There was a man who saw her and with arms outstretched to seize her, he rushed forward. He missed by about an inch, he told the police. On hearing him, she turned her face in his direction and smiled directly at him. And then with her last graceful movement, she jumped, her red sari billowing around her. A beautiful butterfly that within seconds was crushed beneath the metal wheels of the train.

'I pray and pray every day that her soul is now in a happy place.

'It was that man who picked up her bag and handed it to the police. I do know the family were all questioned, which is hardly surprising. I found out later there was another dead wife in the family, a woman who had returned to her country and died mysteriously. And now this, a suicide.

'Those brothers must know now that the police will be watching them for a very long time. So yes, I escaped, but at what price? I didn't save my sister and for that, I will never forgive myself.'

12

There were more than a few seconds of shocked silence after Fareeda had finished her story and I knew without looking round that I wasn't the only one who had tears welling up in her eyes. It was Farah, who even though she was clearly choked up, managed to speak first: 'All the stories we've heard in this room have been sad but yours, Fareeda, is the saddest one of all. I think it has touched every one of us, hasn't it?' She posed the question glancing around at us all and was greeted by stunned nods.

'I have heard there has been more than one woman who, in a similar way to your sister, has committed suicide. What your story has done is told us the reason why, but it is not just us who can now understand, thanks to your sister, far more people will have been made aware of the reasons for those suicides.'

Fareeda looked up at that remark, which gave Denise the opportunity to chime in: 'That must be the reason she didn't write down everything she felt for you to read, Fareeda: it was the Embassy she wanted it delivered to. Her final hope must have been that they would not ignore her letter. Instead there would be steps taken to organise more help for all the women in her position.

'I expect she hoped that in the future the officials in Pakistan would question just what sort of life a middle-aged man who wants to take his very young wife away from her family would be giving her. At least those men would be aware that watchful eyes might be upon them. From what you have told us, it sounds as though she made sure that whoever read her letter understood the reason country girls were chosen: not only would they be young and innocent, but without any family near them, they would be easy to control.

'Since details of her suicide, which included her name and that of her husband, were in the local papers, more people are likely to be on the lookout for women in trouble.'

Only seconds later, Amira, who was looking rather worried, turned towards Denise.

'What I don't want you all to think is that all this cruelty behind closed doors that we have heard about over the last weeks is typical of our culture. We might have some different beliefs, but there are many, many happy marriages.'

'That's true,' said Farah, 'my parents were still very much in love with each other when they returned to Iran. And I was always pretty spoilt by all the males in my family as well as my mother. Which is one of the reasons I don't want any of my husband's family turning up on my family's doorstep. My brothers would simply love to get their hands on the man who had treated me so badly.'

'So they don't know everything?' Denise asked.

'No, just that I've left him and that I'm moving in with some friends.'

'So, when will you see them?' I asked, as I had been wondering what she had planned for her own future.

'I'm leaving it for a year, then that family I married into will perhaps have calmed down.'

'She's right,' Fareeda said, 'not only are there plenty of happy marriages in our culture but also fathers who love and respect their daughters as much as they do their sons. Our parents only agreed to our marriages because they believed we were going to a country where we would have very comfortable lives.

'I did say I'd tell you what my driver told me, didn't I?' Fareeda added. A question we all said yes to and then waited for her to tell us. From the expression on her face we knew this snippet of information would be painful.

'Seems my husband forgot to tell either me or my parents when he asked for my hand in marriage that I was not going to be his first wife. And he was smart enough to choose me, whose family lived in a very different part of Pakistan than the one before so they wouldn't have had any idea that I would be the second wife.'

'So what happened to her?' Denise asked.

'That's what the police wanted to know. The story he put out was that she had gone back to her parents' home and died. A heart condition, it was said. But the police checked the flight and yes, she had flown back with a member of her husband's family.'

'And then she died?'

'She did, but all her family had was the death certificate, she never arrived at their house. So, although the British police were suspicious, their hands were rather tied then. Her family's bank accounts were checked and sure enough, there was a sum of money, which to a poor family, would have appeared large, taken from the bank by the relative who flew with her. The reason given was that it was to pay for the funeral and to compensate them a little for their grief. Of course it was believed that it was used to keep the family quiet, but exhuming the body was not possible then so there is no proof of what they suspected.'

'Sadly, what I've come to realise since I've worked in the refuge is that every country has some men living in it who have no respect for women at all, which all of us in here are far too aware of,' Denise concluded.

'I've worked in this refuge for enough years to know that. When I was first here most of the women who came in were white and British, as were their husbands. Some had been married to wealthy professionals, others to men who worked with their hands. Then there were the husbands who taught in our schools and universities. We had a judge's wife here once and a few from the military and police forces. Men who have no respect and little sense of caring for the women they have lived with come from different cultures. I heard from one woman who came into the refuge in the seventies when they first opened just how many managed to escape their homes and find their place of safety.'

13

Denise told us a couple more stories – I think it was to make sure those who had told their stories took comfort in knowing it was not just men from their culture that caused such misery. When she had finished, I made some more soothing herbal tea then went up to my room, clutching my cup and my baby. She had managed to sleep all the while we were talking, for which I was thankful. Justin was still sprawled out on his little makeshift bed, fast asleep. Not a twitch came from him when I crept into the room as silently as possible.

Luckily, nappy changing is not noisy. A whimper from Jade before I fed her and then she drifted off to sleep, allowing me to pop her into the cot. Drained, I crawled into bed myself.

I cried that night; cried for all the women who had suffered at the hands of those unscrupulous men. But I didn't cry for myself for I had made myself pack my own story firmly away in my memory box. One day I would be ready to open it and then I would deal with everything in order, admit my mistakes and swear never to repeat them. Until then it was to remain closed and would stay in the dark recesses of my mind. That was when I realised that I was ready to leave the refuge and start sorting out my life in the real world outside of its doors.

I thought briefly about the friendly woman from the council who had come to see me during the first week I was in there, who confirmed that I had been placed on what was called the 'emergency housing list'. She had helped me fill in several forms and also made notes for a report on the emotional effects our violent home life had wreaked on Justin. When she eventually gathered up her paperwork, I was reassured that it wouldn't take long before the keys of a new home were handed over to me. That night, I hoped that she would be true to her word – it was time for me to move on. If I was to succeed in giving my children a decent childhood, then I had to stand on my own two feet and get my life sorted out.

Despite this, I couldn't help but feel a huge sadness at the thought of having to say goodbye to the women I had grown to like so very much. They had certainly opened my eyes to just how many of us needed help and that it was there – we only had to ask for it. How I wished I could tell more women who were going through hell that no one has to live in fear. I knew that once I walked back into the outside world, it was very unlikely that I would ever see any of these wonderful women again – they would be sent to different towns for their own protection.

There had been a great comfort in knowing them and they had gone out of their way to help me with my children, which had almost made me feel part of an extended family so I knew I was going to miss them a lot. On the other hand, they had helped me and I had also helped them, all of us gaining strength, which was why Denise had encouraged us to spend time together and tell our stories – it made us feel we were not alone. Being in the refuge also made us feel safe and looked after, but now I really needed to begin to look after myself.

I had a baby still too young to ever remember what had happened and a little boy who was still having nightmares, but I could only hope that eventually the trauma he had been through would become a distant memory. My son also needed to begin to have a normal life. I knew I was a stronger woman than the one who had been brought into the refuge only a few weeks ago. The experience had not just given me a feeling of security, it had given me the friendship of women that I doubt I would ever come to know in other circumstances, although when I was at school, there had been children from many different countries there. The difference was that they had grown up in the UK and the majority of their parents had been brought over when they were little more than children themselves. When I visited their homes I had always been made welcome and had only witnessed happy families, but the women I had encountered in the refuge were the invisible ones who were not really seen as part of our community, and in their company I had come to understand that their wishes and desires were not so very different from ours.

But yes, I told myself, *it was now time for me to leave.*

14

It was only couple of weeks after the evening of sharing our stories when Denise rushed upstairs to tell me that the council was sending a social worker to see me and that her report would support my application to the housing department. Well, that got me excited. Surely there could only be one reason why they had arranged this visit through the housing department: that they were going to offer a place for me and my children to move into? What other reason could there be?

'When is she coming?' I asked, thinking it might be several days away only to be told that it was that afternoon at two. The fact that it was organised through the same person who had made the original appointment to see me was reassuring as well. I thought about the kindly, grey-haired woman who must have been close to retirement and the whole conversation we had had that day. As we sat sipping tea, I had felt then, by the sympathetic expression in her hazel eyes, that mine was not the only disturbing story she had heard. Her job might appear to be mainly filling out forms but I had worked out there was a lot more to it than that – my instinct told me that she wanted to help people like me as much as she could. There was just something about her that made me feel comfortable; I found myself telling her how worried I was by Justin's refusal to speak.

'Everyone tells me that he will talk when he's ready,' I said, 'but no one can tell me just how long that will be.'

'Mmm, not surprised you're concerned. It's not knowing when he will speak that's unsettling for you. I can totally understand that,' she told me.

'It's not only that,' I confided, 'he has terrible nightmares and wakes up screaming. Then there's the bedwetting as well. All these problems began just over a year ago.'

'Is there anything you can put your finger on that might explain what started them?'

'Yes, I think so and I've not stopped feeling guilty about it. I know I should have left Dave much earlier than I did.'

'You're not the only one who has told me that. I've heard that said to me many times over the years since I started doing this job but it's never that easy to pack up and go, is it? Not when you have no family who would help you. And you don't, do you?'

That's a shrewd observation, I thought, wondering how she had worked that one out as I had just answered 'no' when she asked initially about my background. I was extremely grateful that she did not ask me the reason why I had no family for that was something I was not ready to talk about.

'So what is it you believe started his bedwetting and nightmares?'

'Seeing me being hit, I suppose,' I muttered, embarrassed.

'The thing is, up until then he had really loved his father, Dave. He would rush up to him as soon as he heard him coming through the door, even when he was still crawling. When Dave was in one of his good moods, Justin was picked up and swung around in the air, which made him scream with joy. I think Dave loved him as well, but in his own peculiar way. He never gave any thought to how our son was being affected by his temper and the acts of violence towards me. Usually the violence happened when Justin was in bed, but he must have heard the sound of Dave shouting and me screaming in pain. Not to mention the bruises he would have seen on me. One time Justin was actually in the room with us when he witnessed his father hitting me and my poor little boy was so distressed. His eyes were wide with fear as he crawled under the table, shaking.'

'What exactly happened that night to make Dave do that?'

'Well, usually I had fed Justin and put him to bed before Dave came in, but that night he had told us both that he would be back early and we could all eat together.

'"You'd like that, Justin, wouldn't you?" he said, grinning. Justin had wriggled with pleasure and said, "Yes, please, Dad." Almost the whole afternoon Justin kept asking if his dad would be back soon. I might have known that if Dave met up with some of his friends, which he nearly always did, he would not keep his promise and like a lot of evenings, he arrived back late. Our meal had been ready to be put on the table for over an hour when the door crashed open and Dave swept in. He had clearly been drinking and as alcohol made him so unpredictable, I should have been more on my guard.

There was no apology or explanation, in fact he just ignored me. Instead he picked Justin up, planted a loud kiss on his cheek and pushed a large bar of chocolate into his chubby little hand.

'Being a small boy, chocolate made the thought of any other food slip straight from his head. He stood there, eyes wide with pleasure and a big smile on his face, as he eagerly started to peel back the wrapper. I said he should leave it until after he'd eaten – "Don't want to spoil your appetite, do you?" I told him, putting my hand out to take it from him. Sweets before any meal are never a good idea. Justin was always such an obedient child and trying not to look too disappointed, he placed the bar of chocolate in my hand. Well of course I told him he was a very good boy and he could have a piece of it once our meal was over.

'That was when Dave looked at me with such a scowl on his face that I just about shook. I knew what was coming, but before I had time to get away from him, he sprang towards me. After catching hold of my arm in a vice-like grip, he pulled it high behind my back and forced my fingers open. At the same time, he was yelling as loud as he could that I had no right to take away the present he had given his son. His face was twisted into a mask of anger and I'm sure mine was now white with fear at what he might do next. My arm was wrenched up so far, I thought he would break it.

'"Are you telling me what to do in my own home?" he yelled, twisting my arm even tighter. I tried to say no but when he was in such a rage, he never listened.'

'Or he didn't want to?' she suggested.

'Yes, I guess that's the real truth. I can still picture everything that took place that day. How he raised his hand and aimed it straight into my face – the crack must have resounded all through the room. And I know in some way that Justin felt he was to blame and through the ringing in my ears, I could hear his howls.'

'Poor kid, he wouldn't have had a clue why that had happened.'

'That's right. Dave just pushed me away, bent down and picked up the chocolate. I could hear Justin's cries turning to frightened hiccups, and turning my head, I could see the fat tears sliding down his cheeks. I wanted to go to him, to tell him that nothing was his fault, but I knew if I did so, Dave would hit me again and that would be even worse. All I could do was watch as he tried to give the chocolate back to his son. But Justin's hunger for his favourite treat had completely gone and he just shook his head.

'Dave didn't give up though. He knelt down so he was on the same level as his son and in a voice suddenly turned gentle, he said, "Eat it, Justin, it's your favourite. Don't take any notice of your mother, she's always trying to spoil things." My poor boy looked so confused then. His eyes were darting from his father to me, like he wanted me to tell him what to do.'

'He would have been so confused, Ava. He didn't want to make his father angry again and at the same time he didn't want to disobey you. It was a nasty game your partner was playing, using your little boy as a weapon.'

'Well, that certainly made Dave angrier, not just at me

either. Those soft tones of his soon disappeared. Grabbing Justin by the shoulder, he just about spat out the words, "Don't eat it then, you spoilt little Mummy's boy!" I can see him now, his whole body shaking with rage as he turned to me and shouted, "Now look what you've done. Always spoiling things ... You're a selfish bitch, aren't you?" I felt anger rising in me too when I saw Justin's eyes filling with tears again. He managed to say he wanted to go to the toilet, any excuse to get out of the room, and he wanted me to take him even though he was old enough to go on his own.

'"You don't need to go," Dave snapped at him. "And you don't need your mother to take you. Thought you were a big boy now." And it was then that Justin wet himself. I could see it trickling down his legs and the wet patch on his trousers grew bigger. He was so ashamed of himself that the wails came back along with his tears. And his father, who had made him so upset, just looked at him in disgust before telling me to get him changed and that he was going out.

'As soon as the door slammed behind him, I gave a sigh of relief, knelt down and hugged my son. I could feel his heart beating as I held him while the last of his tears wet my shoulder as he rested his head on it.

'"I'm sorry, Mum," he kept whispering but the only comfort I could offer was to keep repeating that none of this was his fault. But nothing I said seemed to convince him that it was not him who had caused all that anger swirling around us. We never did eat that night. Justin was too tired, although I did take a few bits and pieces into him once he was bathed and safely in bed. But he just turned his face to the wall and shook his head when I told him I had brought something nice in for him.

'It was after that episode that Justin tried to avoid his father, which made Dave even more bad-tempered. Of course he blamed me. The atmosphere in the house was really bad and that's when I realised I was pregnant. If I had thought that he would change his behaviour when I told him, I was totally wrong. He had been so happy when he learnt that I was pregnant with Justin and I had hoped he would be again. This time he wasn't, not one bit.

'To make things even worse, that was when Justin's nightmares began. I would jump out of bed the moment I heard his cries to find him sat up in bed, his eyes glazed with fear. He never said what the nightmares had been about, but I could guess – he had heard the shouting and screaming and now he knew what those sounds meant. Dave's only concern was that he didn't like being woken up. God, how he moaned about that! Not once did he think it might have been his fault.'

'No, sociopathic narcissists don't,' I was told. 'And Dave has certainly ticked all the boxes to make me believe that's what he is. Good thing you got away, Ava. Was it around then that Justin stopped talking too?'

'No, it was just after we managed to escape from the house. Justin must have been terrified that I had got out and he was left behind, even if it was only for a short time.'

'Well, it's hardly surprising, is it? A child of four hearing all of that must have been terribly frightened. Not only that, I doubt he even understood why you took his sister and not him when you managed to get out of the house. He was too young to have worked out that you hadn't a choice. It was not the first time he had seen the two people he loved fighting, but that night when you escaped, he saw something he would never be able to understand: his father, the man he had adored, looking as though he was trying to kill his mother. And my colleague's report explained what happened the last time he saw his father: what he saw was the man he had become afraid of, trying to take him away. The man who had shouted at him and called him a mummy's boy. The one who had beaten his mother right in front of him. Most probably he believed the same thing was going to happen to him – that would have increased his fear and made him even more reluctant to talk.'

My social worker then told me that she had come across similar problems in other bewildered small children who had been brought into the refuge with their bruised and battered mothers but given time, those memories grow dim – 'and with good, devoted mothers like you, a happy child gradually reappears. We will keep an eye on him and have him assessed by the child psychologist as soon as you are settled, so try not to worry too much, Ava. As everyone has told you, Justin will talk when he wants to.'

'You mean when he finally feels safe?'

'Yes, but not only that, it's also when nice things happen, which he will store in his mind, that he will begin to erase the bad memories.' She sounded so kind and understanding as she said this, giving my hand a light pat. Little wonder I liked her and it was after this conversation that I began to feel more positive about the future.

Following our meeting, she explained, she would write her report, recommending an urgent placement away from the refuge. She asked if there were any areas I would be reluctant to be moved to. My answer to that had been as long as it wasn't near where Dave or his friends lived, I was all right to move more or less anywhere. She told me that flexibility helped because there was a scarcity of flats and some people were so fussy about where they wished to live that even if it was an emergency, they might be on the council list for months.

'Whereas some people just take the first place they can. So, Ava, I've said that you are on the urgent list and made a note that you will need to be near a primary school but apart from that, you will agree to take any flat that comes up. OK?'

'Yes,' I said. 'Will I have to wait long?'

'No, there are some areas where places come up more quickly than others and before you ask why, it's not because of deaths, in case that's what you're thinking,' she said with a wry smile.

'So what's the reason then?'

'Because there are some council estates where tenants come and go a bit more often than others.'

'Why's that?'

'Because the people who go into them are often like you. They need to get rehomed as fast as possible. Anywhere will do is what they say because again, like you, they want their independence – a new word for them. So many of them have almost forgotten what that feels like. Once some of their confidence returns, they often apply to move to other areas; all for different reasons. Sometimes it's because they have family or friends in other towns and they prefer to be near that support structure. Then there are those who still feel they are too close to the man or family they have escaped from, which makes them want to move as far away as possible. That's quite a common reason. And the ones who are still afraid of their ex-partner do everything in their power to move. Once they succeed, then we have an empty flat or house. And the last reason is if the occupant has been reported more than once for serious breaches of their tenancy; sometimes criminal offences which can mean they are moved, even sent to prison. But don't worry, we will make sure you and the children are placed carefully.'

When we said goodbye, she once again told me not to worry too much. She could tell I was a caring mother and things would turn out all right and that the housing officer, Mrs Williams, would be in touch soon.

15

That next week, as I waited for Mrs Williams to make contact, I was in a state of nerves. *Had I said the right things?* I kept asking myself, *Would I get a place soon? Why hadn't I heard?* But as soon as Farah told me Mrs Williams was there to see me, I could tell by her beaming smile that she had good news for me.

'Yes, Ava, there's a flat – well, it's a maisonette actually, which is even better. Two-bedroom and there's a small garden on the ground floor.' She then said that she had to tell me that this estate was considered a bit rough. A lot of people, perhaps not so desperate as me, had refused it on the grounds that it was not safe for their children.

'How unsafe is it?' I asked anxiously, wondering whether there might be sex offenders and paedophiles who preyed on children.

'Oh, nothing too bad, it's known to have a drug problem,' was her reply. 'Still, that shouldn't bother you, considering the age of your children.'

I gulped at that, thinking of Dave. It would be a huge problem if it was their father who was one of the dealers around there. As if reading my mind, Jill, as she had told me to call her, said hastily, 'I've checked with the police and your ex-partner is definitely not involved in that area's drug problem. They know who the dealers are and they're trying to crack down.'

I was only too aware that the neighbourhood that she had told me about was not the best, but I needed to get my small family into a place where we would be together and safe.

'Sounds all right to me, Jill,' I said firmly. 'Dealers won't pester me too much. All I've got to do is say no. So, is this place already furnished? I know you told me the council would help me sort that out.'

'They do, so as soon as you agree to take it and sign the lease, we'll organise the basics for you. Luckily for us, people often donate their old furniture and then ...' and here she paused a little.

'And then there's the furniture that belonged to those who died with no one to leave it to, that ends up in flats like mine, I suppose?' I added.

'Well, yes. But everything is cleaned thoroughly and done up so it's not that different to shopping in a second-hand shop, is it?'

She went on to say that I would receive unemployment money, child benefits and that my rent would be paid and there would be other help given.

'There's quite a good primary school not that far from the estate, just a bus stop or two away, and there's a good nursery not too far either.'

'So where exactly is it?' I asked and she gave me the

address, which I recognised. It was not far from where Jean lived so at least there would be one person I knew, even if the area was not that great.

Jill's face lit up when I told her that I had a friend who lived nearby.

'One who will be supportive?'

'She absolutely will.'

'Good, because I know you've made friends here and you will miss them when you go. And by the looks of you, the time spent in the refuge has done you the world of good.'

'It has, but you're right, I really will miss the other women here. We've spent so much time together and they've tried their best to help me and my children. I think Justin will miss them too. But still, I've got to sort my life out and make sure that from now on, my kids have as much of a normal life as I can possibly give them. So I'll make the new place into a peaceful home, which will be good for Justin, won't it? Thank goodness my daughter won't remember a thing, but Justin's seen and heard far too much.'

When I told her that, Jill asked if he had started saying the odd word or two.

'No, and my biggest concern is he's due to begin school fairly soon and how will he cope? Who's going to want to play with a little boy who won't speak?'

'Don't you remember what we said, Ava, about taking it one step at a time?'

I smiled at her then.

'I do. Good you reminded me, I've been fretting all night.'

'The teachers will help. It won't be the first time that they've had to deal with a child whose gone through a traumatic experience. And he won't be the only one whose mother has had to escape a violent marriage. Not every child speaks that well when they begin school. Remember, it will be the first day at school for all of them. Plenty of tears and tantrums all round. So I doubt if many would really notice your son's lack of speech.'

I gave a sigh of relief at those words.

'I suppose you're right.'

'I know I am, Ava.' She smiled. 'Years of experience tell me that.'

Jill was so easy to talk to that I decided to bring up another question that I'd been pondering: 'I want to improve my education, but I don't know how to start. Maybe you can give me some advice.'

She looked up at me then, her eyes brightening. It was not a question that had been thrown at her very often, she told me, but she might have some ideas.

'What is it you have in mind?' she asked.

I explained that I'd had a few problems in my past which had affected my schooling. I wanted to retake my GCSEs to improve my grades and then of course it would help me to apply for various jobs.

'I have my children to think of,' I told her. 'I'm going to be the breadwinner for a long time so if I can get myself better-educated, it will help in two ways, won't it?'

'Go on,' she said encouragingly.

'Well, a parent should always set a good example, shouldn't they? And I want my two to understand how important education is. Plus, with some exams under my belt, I'll be much better at helping them with their homework later on, which is so important, don't you think?'

It was a question she didn't answer; instead a warm smile broke out across her face.

'Look, the first step is to get you and the children settled in. The next is to go and see the school head and get Justin into school and to look for a crèche for your daughter. And finally to decide which classes you want to take. Do you know that if you're studying, the council will help with all the crèche fees?'

I didn't, but just that bit of knowledge made me even more determined. I was going to get myself educated, I told myself, and provide a good future for my children.

16

Two days later, I was packed and all ready for the move. Jill Williams, the housing officer, had arranged to take us to our new home as soon as breakfast was over. She had told me that the place could do with some decorating but that it had been cleaned from top to bottom and there was some furniture in it that was not too bad.

'Won't be the first time I've had to make a tatty place look like home,' I'd told her, keeping my fingers crossed that it wouldn't be in too bad a state. I could hardly wait for Jill's arrival, though there was still a part of me that did feel sorry that soon I would have to say goodbye to the friends I had made at the refuge. Naturally I was also wondering how, once I left the security of the refuge, I was going to cope. For the first time in years I would be living in a place without adult company and I told myself, *without anyone bossing you around. You're free again and now you can make your own decisions, cook the food you like and wear whatever you want to, even take a book to bed with you. And of course spend time with your children – that's what single mums do, isn't it?*

Except, I thought, *all the bills are down to one person's income, aren't they? Think back*, my inner voice persisted, *how many times did Dave's money run out and how often did you have to make a meal out of scraps? Well, at least now you'll be in charge of budgeting and you won't have anyone trying to pinch what you had left in your purse either. Now, isn't being a single mum much better than the life you put up with for too many years? The answer to that has to be a yes, though if I hadn't listened to Dave then I would still have a circle of friends who would have rallied round to support me,* I thought sadly. *Still, Jean's going to visit and she's the one who really understands how I came to make those mistakes.*

But however much I told myself that there was nothing to worry about, it didn't stop those little ripples of anxiety running through my mind. Which was not what I wanted my son to see. So, telling myself not to be so silly, I tried my best to get Justin excited about going to our new home.

'Jill's here now,' I told him as through the window I saw the gate opening and her car pulling in. 'Now we're going for a drive so up you get.'

Turning to the friends I had made, I simply said, 'She's arrived now.' My bags were lifted up by them and carried out as they all came out to say their final goodbyes. Outside, Amira handed me a bag filled with the same sweet cookies that had been made for Justin on his first night there. He had certainly tucked into them then and I knew they would compensate a bit for yet another changing situation. The memory of that day when we had first met these women seemed faded, a lifetime away.

Farah gave Justin a hug and then handed him a drawing book – 'You keep working on those pictures you showed me,' she told him – while Fareeda presented me some lovely photos of me with my two children. I would have really liked one of our whole group, but I understood why they thought that might not be a good idea. Once my luggage and my little family were in the car, I was given hugs as my friends wished me good luck for the future and I wished them the same. Then I thanked Denise, who was on duty that day, for all the help she had given me before I too climbed into the car.

Gazing up at them through the window, Justin smiled at all the women, albeit a little dolefully. His mood since being told that this was the day we were going to our new home had fluctuated. I expect, like me, he was nervous about leaving the refuge, a place he had come to feel safe in. Naturally, he had grown fond of the women there who had been so kind and patient with him so I suppose his lack of excitement about this, our latest move, was hardly unexpected.

'Best stop and get you stocked up,' said Jill, pulling up in front of a large supermarket after a while.

Good thing I'd made a list of essentials or we would never have been back in the car in less than thirty minutes.

Once we were on our way again, I felt myself growing impatient to see the place where we were going to live, even though Jill had warned me that it was not in the best shape – not that she gave any reason for it then. A few minutes later, Jill took a left turning and told me we had reached the estate. I could see at one glance that she was right about the area. Whatever the estate had once looked like over the years since it had been built, it had definitely gone to seed. As she pointed out, three decades of wear had taken their toll. Paint blistered by the seasons was peeling off windows and door frames, some gardens looked cared for while others were overgrown with coarse grass and dead bushes, net curtains hung drably from many of the windows and hid the interiors from passers-by and after we took another turning, we drove past backyards where cats sat comfortably on walls and damp washing flapped in the breeze.

Jill chatted away about how, when the second part of the estate was being built, she had just begun work with social services and had seen the first families move in. Though then, it was not that many years after the first refuge had opened in London and seeing the need for them, more began opening their doors in different areas: 'That's why I saw a lot of the estate when I was given the job to accompany women and children to one of these flats. They were a little luckier back then with their housing. Nearly every house that I went into smelt of new paint. Still, I've noticed today that quite a few of the gardens have been looked after, which is good. In those days it was just freshly dug soil but those first tenants were so thrilled at having a brand-new home and within a few weeks, they had planted shrubs and flowers. They were so full of optimism when they were handed their keys. Things have changed over the years, though. When I began working there was far less of a shortage of affordable homes. This estate had a youth centre and it's a great shame it's gone now.'

On hearing this, I caught sight of a few bored-looking teenagers, kicking a football around lethargically.

'Here we are,' Jill announced as she pulled up in front of a red-brick building at the end of a terrace of small houses.

When Justin heard those words, he stared out of the window, looking to see what his new home was like. Jade, meanwhile, barely stirred. Between us, we managed to unload all our baggage and the children, although I had the uncomfortable feeling that there were several pairs of eyes watching us – 'Probably wondering what their new neighbours are like,' Jill said when I mentioned it to her.

As I looked at the windows of the flat I was moving into, I noticed the concrete staircase at the side of the building which led to the upstairs flat – well, at least we only had to walk to the front door, which I felt was a bit of good luck.

'Our new home, Justin,' I told him, not that he gave me a reply. 'Just look around a bit and once we're inside, you can explore.' As I said this, I saw his lips quiver and I could tell he was still a little uneasy. I wondered if he was thinking that his dad might turn up there – that thought would have been enough to frighten him. 'Going to be just the right size for us three,' I added quickly, hoping the word 'three' would reassure him. And then, carrying Jade and our luggage between us, we made our way up the path to our new front door.

Jill handed me the key: 'I think you'd better unlock your own front door,' she said with a smile. And with one click it opened and I stepped inside. Jade, who had seemed to be asleep, opened her eyes, kicked her legs out and gurgled away as if saying hello to her new home.

Dropping my case onto the floor, I cast my eyes around the living room as my nostrils filled with an aroma I immediately recognised – bleach. It seemed every inch of the place had been scrubbed with it. *That smell tells a story*, I thought to myself, wondering if the people who had lived there had been the ones who had to be removed. Maybe that's why I got such a suspicious look from my new neighbour who was sitting on the top step of the staircase to the upper flat when we walked in. Just how bad had this place been before the cleaners arrived, I was tempted to ask. If this flat had been as filthy as I imagined it must have been to require dousing with bleach, then they had hardly been the sort of neighbours anyone would have wanted to live near.

Our new home might have looked and smelt clean, but with the peeling wallpaper and dark cracked and worn lino, these were the best things I could say about it.

'Doesn't look like the previous tenants had any plans to turn this place into a comfortable home,' I noted.

Jill, who I was pretty sure never repeated much of what took place in her job, must have had a good reason for what she told me next. I have to say that it was her explanation that in a way changed my life: 'Oh, I might as well tell you, because you'll hear all about what happened in no time at all. They were drug dealers and not small fry either. Not that they were here to sell drugs themselves but they wanted to recruit young teenagers from the area to do it for them. Once that was done and the dealers were satisfied that they had a decent grip on their latest recruits, they would move on, leaving these brain-addled kids fast becoming addicted to the drugs they were selling. One man would stay behind until he had found a couple of tough older boys he could leave in charge, ones that the new recruits would be scared of. Scared enough that if they were picked up by the police, getting information out of them would be nigh on impossible – not that they ever really knew much. And that's how it's done, Ava. Which is the major reason the police are seldom able to track down the big people, who almost certainly live an apparently respectable and affluent life in one of our cities.

'So, how did they get this flat? The answer is that they didn't. What those men do is look for vulnerable people and then think of different ways of moving in. Better to get a feel of the territory by living close to it for a while but even more importantly, they want to remain anonymous. In this case your flat was occupied by a single mother. She had two young children, not that it stopped her helping them. I would guess that the moment the smell of money was dangled under her nose she opened the door to them. To the people on the estate they were just friends of hers but someone saw through them fairly quickly. Not every young teenager wants to be a dealer, thank goodness. And few parents want to raise a future addict either. The drugs they had in their possession when the police raided the flat were ones that cause a very rapid addiction and changes in personality. Those who become addicted to the more dangerous Class A drugs are far more likely to get into crime and often become violent, not that these sorts of people care one iota about ruining young lives. Luckily, the community round here is more tight-knit than they understood and more than one person talked. It's no secret to anyone on the estate what was happening. Their curtains must have been twitching away when they saw the flashing blue lights of the police cars. Fingers must have been crossed in more than one house that the arrests made led to others. Anyhow, I'm sure your neighbours will tell you all about it. There was more than just drug dealing, which you will doubtless hear about as well, but it's not my place to tell you anything else.'

'I suppose that explains a bit about the state the place was in, though you'd think they might have been more careful. Still, it's a good thing I'm used to decorating. When I moved in with Dave, I really transformed the place, making it light and airy. We must have spent all our time peeling away endless layers of wallpaper and painting, I even learnt a bit of plastering. That was at the beginning of our relationship, when I still thought he was wonderful,' I said sadly. 'Still, it's a new life now, one with just me and the kids. And if I've transformed one flat, I can do it again.'

'That's the spirit, Ava,' she said encouragingly.

Yes, that *was* the spirit, but what I didn't tell her was that as she spoke I had made a momentous decision: this flat was going to be a temporary home. By the time my children had reached senior school age, I was somehow going to move them to a safer place. The police might have got rid of one lot of dealers, but that didn't mean that there wouldn't be replacements. Which, having lived with one estate like that, I was pretty certain there would be, as estates such as these are fertile ground for dealers. Though to be fair to Dave, he wasn't selling that sort of drugs to underage children, as Jill had described. He was catering more for the party- and club-goers. Even so, his reputation was that of a dealer and with no man in the house to protect them, my two children could easily become targets for other dealers. For from what my housing officer had told me, it was the families of poorer, single mums that those unscrupulous dealers would be on the lookout for.

Listening intently to every word she told me had made me very determined to ensure that nothing like that would ever happen to my children. Somehow, before they were senior school age, I would move my family to a safer place. One in a completely different area where no one would know what their father did for a living. Which did not mean that for the time we lived in the flat, I would not make it as homely as possible. The good thing about the place was even though it was beyond tired, the furniture the council had put in was not too bad. A dark blue settee and matching chair were both completely stain-free if a little shabby, but some upholstery shampoo and a few bright throws would sort that out. There was a dark oak table and three rather battered wooden dining chairs. As for the curtains – horrible thin, shiny and grimy fabric in a shade of dull green – my fingers itched to pull them down. I got the feeling they had been in the flat since the first tenant moved in.

A double bed was in the reasonable-sized bedroom and there were bunk beds in the smaller one. The mattresses were new and still in their plastic wrapping. 'Be a long time before Jade can use one of them,' I said. But good they had thought towards the future, I suppose. Justin was already trying to clamber up to the top bunk. There was one chest of drawers. *I need to get some money together to add a few more things*, I thought. *Scour the charity shops … A couple of bright mats would also make it appear better.*

As for the walls, there was a bit more needed than paint. All that horrid wallpaper would have to be stripped off and a few huge holes filled in before a paintbrush touched them. Jill had already handed me some vouchers, which she told me would cover the cost of paint for the living room.

When I had escaped from Dave, of course I hadn't prioritised pots and pans on my list of necessities so I was thankful to see there were plenty in the kitchen and it was surprisingly clean. The stove hardly looked as though it had been used much too, which told me that the previous tenants must have been living on takeaways.

'I think you'll be all right here, Ava,' Jill repeated. 'I can see you're already looking at how you can make improvements. The department delivered the fridge this morning too, so that's one thing you don't have to try and buy.'

She told me she would call round in a few weeks to see how I was getting on. No sooner had she gone than I started putting everything I had brought with me in the right place. I had just turned on the kettle when I heard a bold knock on the door. Opening it, I grinned with delight when I saw Jean's face beaming back at me.

'Thought I'd better be your first guest,' she told me, dumping a bag in my hands. 'Brought some lunch for all of us. Rotisserie chicken, coleslaw, salad and some nice crusty bread plus some ice cream for you, Justin. So, we can all have a picnic here.' And a bottle of sparkling wine came out of her handbag. 'Put it all in the fridge, Ava, and we can celebrate your moving in a bit later. I want to have a good look around first.'

Having Jean back in my life made me feel really pleased that

I had moved so close to her and after seeing the place with its peeling wallpaper and damaged flooring, she told me my luck was in as she had a steamer, which meant getting off all that wallpaper would be easy. 'And I've got some rolls left over from when I did up my place, so we can paper some of the walls. Once you get the paper off and fill in those holes you can decide on paper or paint. We'll get the place decorated in no time, you'll see. It will make all the difference to the rooms, it's going to look fresh and clean,' she said brightly before suggesting a few colours. It was a pale cream I had already decided on – light colours would make it all appear bigger and lighter.

'Then I can browse through the junk shops and look for pictures to hang on them. Amazing what can be found there. And as for those kitchen units, let's paint them a light blue. They'll look quite different then,' I told her excitedly.

Jean promised to bring the steamer and all her decorating stuff so we could start on it in the morning. Although I had put on a brave face for Jill and I was grateful for everything she had done for me, I was so glad I didn't have to face this next stage on my own.

17

Early the next day, Jean appeared with everything she had promised to bring. After a quick cup of tea, we started work. Justin seemed to think that the job of helping to peel off the wallpaper was great fun. He kept grinning away, which again made me feel he was making some progress. Of course Jade was no problem – she just sat wide-eyed, propped up in a play-pen that Jean had given me.

'Don't know why, but I never threw it out. Wasn't as though I was ever going to need it again,' Jean said in an apparently casual way. It was a remark that made me feel a little sad for her. After her partner's terrible death, she had told me that she would never again let another man into her life. It seemed she had stuck to that decision. So, with my baby keeping herself amused with her toys and watching us from her small playpen and Jason gleefully tearing off wallpaper, we all worked hard on what Jean had now dubbed 'Project Flat Transformation'.

By coffee time we had made a pretty good start. What really surprised me though was when my second visitor, the neighbour from upstairs, arrived a couple of days later just as the last scrap of wallpaper was being removed from the lounge. She was the one I had thought looked so unfriendly when we arrived but there she was at my door, which I had left open to try and get the flat aired because of all the steam and the lingering smell of bleach. She was holding a tray with a can of fizzy drink for Justin, a large pot of tea and a plate with an assortment of biscuits and slices of cake.

'Thought you could do with this while you're busy making this flat look so smart. Anyway, it's a good excuse to come over and say hello.'

I invited her to come in and sit down and Jean got extra mugs, milk, sugar and teaspoons from the kitchen. She was right: a break was exactly what we needed and Jason's little hand was already stretched out towards the tray.

'I'm Hils, by the way,' she told us. 'And you, little man, what's your name?' she asked, turning to Jason. When he just stared at her, I quickly made the introductions.

'In case you're wondering,' my new neighbour told me, 'I'm called Hils because it's short for Hilary but it's the wrong name for someone like me. Makes me think of hockey fields and posh girls running with their sticks clasped in their hands. Who knows what my mum was thinking of? I mean, do I look like a posh schoolgirl?'

With her bleached blonde hair and Northern accent, she had a point.

'No, not really,' I managed to interject.

'I'll take that as a compliment then,' she said, smiling. 'Now I expect you've heard something about how this place became free?'

'A bit,' I said before pausing to find out more. Jean was looking on eagerly too.

'Oh, it was real dramas! Haven't seen so much excitement for years. The whole estate must've been looking out of their windows when the police cars arrived, with their flashing lights and sirens. Dare say a few of them were wondering who'd been up to mischief this time. I guessed just who they were after though and when they pulled up outside and started hammering loudly on the door, I knew that I was spot-on. I thought they were going to break the door down and for once, I felt like cheering the police. Couldn't help going out myself to see what was happening.

'Let's just say I was really happy to say goodbye to that shifty lot and so was just about everyone round this part of the estate. Not that they had much choice, seeing as they were dragged out and just about thrown into police cars. Another car with two social workers inside took the children, poor little mites they were. What goings-on they must have witnessed. Thankfully, those kids were going to be taken somewhere safe – I think the social workers may already have had foster families lined up for them.'

'So, what had been happening?' Jean asked.

'To begin with, the children had a bad mother who neglected them. They were scrappy little things, with dirty clothes and pale faces. She was a single mum and I knew that she left them alone a lot. Down the pub, she was, most evenings and then once she'd found a man to take back home, she would stagger back here. No one knew if she was charging for it, but we all wondered cos you never saw the same fella twice.

That was bad enough, but those dealers she had in her flat made things much worse. God knows what was happening up there – I heard the shouting one night and then the high-pitched screams of those kiddies. That was when I decided to report them.'

What had taken her so long? Somehow, I managed to stop myself from asking that. I could see Jean was struggling too, but we sat back and continued to listen to her story.

'I'd seen the bruises on their mother's face more than once, but did I care? As far as I was concerned, it was up to her how she chose to live her life. But when I saw the bruises on the kids' legs and arms, I knew that fists had been raised to them and that was too much. That's when I got myself down to the station to make a statement, got a few others to back up my story as well. Not that they knew I was the one who shopped them. Between us, we were able to give the police information about how these vile people were trying to get teenagers into their web too. OK, this estate might look a bit rough and we turn a blind eye to a lot that goes on, but not when it comes to cruelty to children or trying to turn them into addicts.'

'Those dealers will serve time, but I doubt the mother will,' Jean noted gravely. 'Just hope her kids are never returned to her.'

'Don't think they will be,' said Hils before turning to me. 'Ava, that Jill who brought you over, she's much tougher than she looks. She was one of the two social workers in that car with the kids and she'll be giving evidence. She'll want the mother moved out of this area. So, it looks like a major trouble has gone from this place now – at least until someone new arrives. Anyhow, you don't look like you're here to cause problems, I guess you've had enough of your own.'

'So, you know Jill?' I asked.

'Well, I know who she is and the good work she does,' Hils told me. 'She's a decent sort, all right.'

On hearing all this, I could see no point in pretending that I was just someone who'd been on the council list for a while. It took a little effort to admit that I'd been in a refuge but I was pretty sure that Hils had worked it out anyway. I told her how kind and supportive Jill had been when we met at the refuge.

'Oh, I knew straight away when I saw you turn up with her, but it was up to you if you wanted to let me know. I would never have asked,' I was reassured.

A statement that made me like her even more.

'And your little boy's been through a lot too, I expect. I've seen troubled children before but with mums like you, they recover pretty fast.'

I'd never expected a 'welcome to the estate' visitor, but meeting Hils made me feel that maybe, just maybe, I was going to enjoy living there after all. I felt that day was the start of us becoming friends – and I was right.

I was surprised when later she told me that she also wanted to start her education again. So, I was not the only one who was keen to improve my education and take the various exams I'd not been in a position to sit when I was sixteen. It turned out Hils' father had been an alcoholic who never allowed her the peace to study – 'He just wanted me to leave school at fifteen, get a job and pay for my keep. And Mum was too scared of his temper to stand up for me. Well, he was a bit handy with his fists so I could understand that. I kept telling her to leave him but for some reason, she didn't want to. Anyhow, I decided to leave school the moment I could and then I packed my bags and got out of the house pretty sharpish. Seeing how I wasn't earning much in my first job, I'd been lucky to get a flat share.

'And what about you, Ava, did you study?' she asked.

'No, I didn't get any qualifications either,' I told her. 'Same reason as you more or less.'

'Trouble at home?'

'You could say that.'

And Hils, being Hils, just nodded and left it at that.

It was when the second cup of tea was being poured that I told her about the conversation I'd had with Jill and how she'd given me all the information about a scheme called Access.

'It means adults can have access to education,' I explained. 'There are all types of courses for people who want to take exams they either failed at school or for some reason beyond their control were unable to take. Sounds like we have a really good council in this area, too. They seem determined to help those of us who missed out when we were younger. With those qualifications, we can apply for better jobs in the future and for us women, especially us single parents, it means we will feel a lot more independent and able to come off benefits. I know the council will help with the cost of childcare, even small babies can be placed in a nursery.'

'So, have you applied yet, Ava?' Jean asked. 'Sounds right up your street.'

'No, not yet. I can't help feeling my daughter is too young to be separated from me. After all, she's only a few months old. I know I need to get on with my life, but what's a few more months? I thought I'd at least wait until she was a year old.'

'Yes, but if you're not careful, you'll be saying you'll wait until she's at least two,' Jean warned. 'Time to bite the bullet, my friend. After all, you've already decided you need to sort out your education for the sake of your kids, haven't you?'

'OK, Jean, enough now! I admit you have a point,' I said, feeling increasingly uncomfortable at the direction the conversation was taking.

'I have indeed, Ava. Don't you agree, Hils?' she persisted.

'I think she has to decide what's best for her family, Jean,' Hils said thoughtfully. 'But, Ava, I do know something about the nursery you mentioned. Some of my friends kids went there when they were only babies and from everything I've heard, it's a really good place. And you know that Jill would never have recommended it, given what she does?'

'True,' I agreed.

'There's a reason the council helps pay the cost of childcare for babies as young as Jade when their mums are working hard to improve their education. Once they've enrolled, they know that it's the first step towards planning their future. And let's face it, Ava, she wouldn't have given you all that information if you hadn't shown any interest. It's just that you don't want to part with Jade for several hours a day, isn't it?' Hils mused.

'Mm … I suppose you're both right and I know what you're going to say next: it's me that will miss her, not the other way round, isn't it?'

Jean grinned at me. 'You've got that bit right! Look,

I understand that most mothers would like to stay at home until their kids are in senior school but that doesn't work for single mums, does it? And children, however young, well they adapt quickly to new routines, usually quicker than their mums. So at least take yourself off to the nursery and have a good look at the happy little faces you will see in there.'

'OK, you two win. I'll go there and see how it's run but I have to make sure my son is settled and happy in his school first. I've already got an appointment with the Head. I'm just hoping he'll be OK there, he's been through so much.'

'I could put money on it,' Hils told me. 'Kids need stimulation at that age and they need to start making friends. The Head has a great reputation and I'm sure you'll find she gets it totally and she's completely understanding and helpful.'

She ruffled Justin's hair, smiled down at him and told him it was a lovely school and he would soon have lots of new friends to play with. Having become used to the women at the refuge, he smiled back at her.

I asked where the nursery was and it turned out that it was in the opposite direction to the school. Yes, there was a bus that went just about to the door, but that still meant extra bus fares each day.

After picking up the tray and empty plate, my new neighbour said her goodbyes, adding that she hoped we might all become friends. Jean and I smiled at her warmly.

After she left, Jean got a notepad out of her bag and started listing the various tasks we had agreed on.

'So, Step One, see the Head and get Justin started at his new school. Step Two, visit the nursery ...' Which made us glance down at the cushion where Jade was lying peacefully. 'But the really important one is Step Three: enrol in some suitable courses for yourself. OK, Ava? And I can help by babysitting the kids so you can talk to the Head alone.'

I accepted gratefully, knowing it would make a difficult meeting a little easier.

Jean tore the page from her notepad and placed it on the kitchen worktop. After that, we went back to work, but still the thought of having to struggle for money worried me. Not that we were rolling in it when I lived with Dave. There were times when like many others in my situation I had to resort to food banks and I shopped in charity shops a lot. But I didn't want Justin going to school in shabby clothes – he was beginning to grow and it was difficult to keep up. I told myself that somehow we'd manage.

There was no going back now ...

18

Jean, as good as her word, arrived about the same time as my alarm woke me on the day of my meeting with the Head. It had taken me ages to go to sleep the night before but I was in a deep sleep when the alarm and the doorbell sounded, one after the other.

'I'll sort out your two, just get yourself ready,' was her greeting when, a bit blurry-eyed, I opened the front door to her. *Today is Step One, so let's be positive*, I told myself as I got ready to go to the school. I think being a little nervous about meeting the Head was pretty normal. After all, she was going to need me to give some explanation as to why my son was still refusing to speak. The teacher in charge of the new beginners' class would also need to know why so she could help him. So, making a good impression had to be important, didn't it? That's what I told myself as after a quick shower, I began rummaging through the clothes that hung on my newly purchased dress rail.

'Want my advice?' asked Jean, who holding a cup of tea in

one hand and a plate with slices of toast and Marmite in the other, had just put her head round the door.

'Might be a good idea, I can hardly find anything smart.'

'Then jeans and this white shirt,' she said firmly as she pulled the hanger off the rail. 'That's a good outfit for a busy mum. Just tie your hair back, don't bother with much make-up, a little mascara and some lip gloss will do.'

'OK, Jean, and thanks,' I said as following her instructions, I quickly pulled on the only pair of decent denims I had and the white shirt that Jean had already placed on the bed. I made sure my hair was tied back neatly, put on a little bit of make-up, not that I ever wore much anyhow. Now I was ready. I sat on my bed and sipped my tea, although I didn't know how I was going to swallow the toast, I was still so nervous. *Better had*, I told myself. *Don't want a rumbling stomach in the middle of an interview, now do we?* Not that forcing myself to eat stopped me from worrying about the questions I might be asked, like how long was it since Justin had talked. The Head had already been told that he was neither deaf nor dumb, just that he had stopped talking. Although my housing officer Jill Williams had arranged everything with the school, I was pretty sure she would not have given the reasons for Justin's silence.

The Head was bound to want to know how wide a vocabulary Justin had when he was talking and I expected her to ask me for the details of what had happened to make him stop speaking. Then I would have to explain just what had caused a bright little boy who less than a year ago had chattered away non-stop to become completely speechless.

Which would mean me telling her about that last row; the one where I had managed to get out with my baby and me covered in blood, but not taken him. That was a subject I really didn't want to get into. Just thinking about that terrible day almost drowns me in guilt. I knew, and so would she, that it was that act of abandonment which had caused his refusal to speak. I can remember exactly how I felt when I was safely in the doctor's rooms – guilty as hell. Justin had been terrified, I knew – he had not moved an inch when right in front of him his father, who he adored, appeared to be intent on killing me.

It might have been a stroke of luck that just before Dave managed to attack me again, I had managed to get out, but still, I had left my bewildered little boy in the same room as a violent and unpredictable man, bellowing out his rage. Dave's shouting out his threats of what he would do to me if I didn't come back were so loud, everyone in the street could hear him. The question that has been in my mind ever since that day was what would have happened to Justin had the police not arrived so quickly. Although the sound of the police, who his father had always called his enemies, hammering on the door, must have frightened Justin even more. And just how had he felt when they stomped in and dragged his father out of the house?

I hope he felt he was safe when a woman he had never met before took hold of his hand and brought him to me. As I sipped my tea, I could still almost feel the tremors running through his small body as I knelt on the floor when he came through the surgery door and wrapped my arms around him. How many times had I told myself that I had no other choice but to get out of the house? But I still felt I was more than partly to blame for the effect it had had on my son. After all, it wasn't the first time he had heard me screaming in pain when Dave's fist connected with my body. Those thin walls of his bedroom would scarcely have muffled my cries.

The Head would have had a pretty good idea that the row had not been an isolated event so wouldn't she want to know what the last straw had been? She might think I wasn't a fit mother. *That's complete nonsense, Ava,* I told myself. *He would have been removed if you were and it's your son you have to think about now. If you don't pull yourself together, you'll be late for your appointment,*' my inner voice said snippily. *What she thinks of you doesn't matter, what's important is how they deal with him.*

Picking up my bag and after checking in the mirror that I had no toast crumbs on my face, I drew my shoulders back, kissed my children goodbye, thanked Jean again and headed off.

* * *

When I met the Head I was in for a pleasant surprise. Instead of the stern-faced woman I had pictured in my mind, I was greeted by a woman with spikey short dark hair and large blue eyes, who was instantly friendly. 'You must be Ava,' she said as she came up to me. 'I'm Helen.' The smile she gave me lit up her face. Gone were the days when Heads looked formal, I realised, taking in her blue-and-white top and wide-legged navy trousers.

'I expect you could do with a coffee, I know I need one,' was the next thing she said to me as she showed me into her office.

'I could do with one too, thank you so much,' I said, which was rather an understatement. As I walked into her bright and colourful office I felt nearly all that tension and doubt leaving me. The chair she pointed to was not the formal one opposite her desk but a more casual one by a small coffee table, which was far less intimidating.

'I'm a bit of a coffee-holic,' she admitted as she poured out two cups from a filter jug. Feeling some of my confidence returning, I decided to stop worrying about how she might respond and just let the truth flow out.

In fact, her way of asking about Justin's problem was done so tactfully that I felt comfortable telling her what our life had been like before and after we were taken to the refuge.

'Seems like both of you had a pretty rocky time,' was her sympathetic response. She asked how I was coping now I had left the refuge, which told me that I really had been worrying about nothing: she certainly had no intention of firing questions at me, or so it seemed. The only difficult question she asked me was what Justin's speech had been like before that horrible event.

'Oh, he loved chatting,' I told her. 'There would be a wide smile on his face as he talked non-stop and even though he was still little, I could understand just about every word he said.'

'I'm sure you miss that a lot, Ava,' she said.

As I nodded that I did, suddenly I felt the prickling of tears behind my eyes and swallowed hard. Strange, isn't it, how unexpected kindness can bring them on?

'Try not to worry too much, Ava,' the Head continued. 'I'm pretty certain he will be talking again soon. He's not the first child that's come to this school with problems. Just being with the other pupils will help and our teachers are trained to help children who have been through trauma.'

There was not a hint of her attempting to criticise me. In fact, she told me it was clear that I was a good mother who put her children first. Helen also reassured me that Justin wouldn't be picked on because he wasn't talking.

'Some of his age group don't say much straight away. After all, a new environment away from home is daunting for all the children. His teacher will keep an eye on him and encourage him to play games. I'd be surprised if he isn't talking again well before he leaves the infant class. Let me say again that we've had other children here who have gone through major trauma, before or after they start here. They are usually very shy to begin with but with our help, it's only a matter of weeks before their confidence returns. Basically, what we try and do is fill up their days with some fun activities, then gradually their new memories begin to push the bad ones away.'

'Yes, I've also been told that a few times and I've worked on it as much as possible for myself and the children.'

'Well, trust me, Ava, it does work given time. And we do have child psychologists to call on if we feel the child still needs it, but that is very rare.'

Helen then asked me what interests Justin had and so I told her about his drawings. And I explained that before that last scene he had witnessed, he had been a curious little boy, always asking questions.'

'That's good, Ava, it means his curiosity will eventually make him talk so let's get him started here as soon as possible. Bring him along this coming Monday and his teacher will make sure he sits next to the right child. And I'm sure he will start enjoying being here.

'Anyway, it's been really nice meeting you, Ava,' she said, holding out a hand and then squeezing mine reassuringly.

I thanked her then and as I walked away, I felt lighter: another worry had floated away.

19

That first day when I took Justin to school, I was even more of a bundle of nerves than the morning when I met the Head and however much Helen had tried to reassure me that it wouldn't take long for him to feel at ease there, I couldn't stop worrying. And when we have a worry spinning around in our heads, we hardly have a good night's sleep, do we? It seems as if the dark makes a niggling little worry grow out of all proportion. As I tossed and turned, all I kept asking myself was just how was my silent boy going to cope. I pictured a classroom full of confident little ones, all chattering away and him not being able to join in. I imagined him being mocked and pushed about, for small children are not always kind, are they? And would he be wondering why he had to be there? Maybe he'd start thinking I had abandoned him again. Those were just a few of the fears swimming in my mind that had kept me awake until the early hours.

The moment my alarm went off and I jumped out of bed, I made myself appear bright and happy. *Keep smiling, Ava,* I told myself, as I got my children dressed, fed Jade and made

Justin his breakfast. I kept telling him what a good time he was going to have at school and how he would soon make lots of friends there. His response was to turn his big eyes in my direction and I could see by his expression that I was not the only one who was a little scared about his first day at school. Somehow he managed to eat most of his breakfast but not with much enthusiasm and then it was time to get his jacket on, put Jade in her sling and make our short journey to the school.

'Jade and I will be waiting at the gate for you as soon as school is over,' I told him more than once, which did bring a half-hearted smile to his face. I just wished I could add, 'and then you can tell us all about your day,' but I swallowed those words. Instead, I told him that I thought he would be doing some drawings as, with the baby perched comfortably in her sling and me holding his hand, we walked to the bus stop.

Once we were on the bus I could see I was not the only parent taking their offspring to the school. There was another woman around my age sitting several seats from me. Next to her was a pretty blonde-haired little girl, who I guessed must be somewhere between the ages of six and seven. She was looking up at her mother, who was smiling down at her and from the way their lips moved, I could tell they were talking quietly to each other. My heart sank – I would have given anything to be able to hear my son's voice again. And the question that kept coming into my mind was, would I ever? Everyone I had spoken to about it, including a paediatrician, had told me he would talk again in his own time; all I could do was hope that they were right.

There were only three stops and then we got off the bus and began walking the short distance to the school. The mother of the little blonde girl caught up with us and introduced herself as Stella. Her daughter was called Annie.

'I don't think I've seen you before, have I?' she asked.

'Oh, I've just moved into the area, so it's my son's first day here,' I said airily, crossing my fingers that Annie would not try to speak to Justin. I really didn't want to tell someone I hardly knew that he was not using his voice at the moment, let alone the reasons why. Though I suppose I could have just pretended that he was shy. Luckily, Annie was too busy calling out to one of her friends to be bothered trying to get to know a small boy who was younger than her.

Having to join a group of mothers saying goodbye to their children was another thing I hadn't thought about. There was a big group of them by the school gates and they all seemed to know each other. Somehow, I had to walk through those gates to take Justin in to meet his teacher. I was nervous enough about leaving him there and I just didn't want to get into any more conversations, no matter how friendly. The trouble was that they seemed a welcoming bunch who immediately wanted to include me in their conversation. Smiles came in my direction and one remarked what a good-looking boy Justin was. I smiled at that and squeezed his hand. A few questions came my way and I gave the same responses I had given Stella.

Please don't ask me where I've moved from, I begged silently. *Or why I'm here, or anything about Justin's father*. To my relief, none of them did. Later, when I did get to know a couple of them a little better, it turned out that I was not the only mother they had met who had to escape a violent husband so they knew better than to ask too many questions apart from the names of the children.

Still holding Justin's hand, I made my excuses and walked up to the school entrance. A young teacher, with a mass of streaky blonde hair and a round, pretty face, smiled broadly as she knelt down to introduce herself to Justin: 'Hello, my name is Sally and you're called Justin, aren't you?' This won her a nod and a slight smile in return. She told us both that he was going to enjoy his first day and that she was going to make sure he did; she had heard he liked drawing so that was something he would be doing. Then she held her hand out for him to take, which to my amazement he did, and led him into the classroom. Nice as I thought she was, it did not stop a lump rising in my throat as they disappeared through the doors. This was the first time we had been separated for any length of time since he had been born and I found it hard to fight back the tears. Naturally, I also found it hard to relax that day as all the thoughts that had kept me awake came drifting into my mind again. I must have paced around that flat all day with my eyes constantly checking the time and I couldn't stop wondering if Justin was all right. Surely if he had got too upset then the school would be ringing me? But no phone call came.

I was certainly the first person to be at the school gates at the end of that day, waiting anxiously to see how he was when his class came out. Other mothers gradually appeared and one, seeing the anxious look on my face, said, 'Oh, the first day we have to leave our children is always a little worrying, isn't it? I know I felt really tearful. And then we end up finding out that they've had such a good time, they didn't miss us one bit.'

'I so hope that's the case with my little boy,' I said.

'Oh it will be, you'll see,' she told me reassuringly.

Which I did see when he came out with a group of other small children. Not a tear in sight, they ran up to their mothers. My son, who was smiling broadly when he saw me, was in their midst. His teacher came out to talk to me: 'He's been really good,' she told me. 'Drawing away. He's got talent, hasn't he? I put his picture up on the wall and he was so pleased. I have to say, he's a credit to you. He's so well behaved, I really enjoyed having him in my class.'

Hearing that, I could feel myself welling up.

So that's Step One completed, I told myself as we returned home. *And now for Step Two …*

20

To my surprise it seemed to take less than a week for me to see that Justin was actually enjoying school. His refusal to talk didn't appear to make much difference to the other children in his class. Each afternoon when I went to pick him up, he rushed towards me with a big grin on his face. And what really made me happy was, as we were beginning to walk to the bus stop, I was seeing him turn around and wave at a couple of small boys. Even better was how, with equally big smiles on their faces, they waved back at him; Justin managing to make friends was just what I had hoped for, although I hadn't thought it would happen so quickly. It meant that he had settled into the school and as the teacher had told me, he was enjoying the whole experience. I finally began to feel far more relaxed; it also meant that was the completion of Step One.

The next thing I had to do was visit the nursery and commence Step Two but the doubts I had had about putting Jade there had not gone away completely. If I was going to go ahead with those classes, I really didn't have another option. I felt it was important to set a good example to my children and

I didn't want them to be like others I had known, who saw no point in studying hard and taking exams. Still, this was not going to be an easy decision and I hated the thought of missing so much of my small daughter's early development – what if she crawled or made her first attempts to stand without me being there? But I realised that I was running out of time. Access would be starting their new courses in just a few weeks and as my new neighbour Hils had said, I needed to have Jade enrolled and settled by then.

To put my mind at rest, I needed to see how the nursery was run. Maybe to begin with I could let her go for just a couple of days to see how she got on. I hoped that when I picked her up she would be the contented and gurgling little baby I needed her to be, for without that could I really go ahead? But as Jean had said, I needed to bite the bullet and organise her going there in the first place.

So, I made my appointment to take Jade to the nursery – 'just for a day,' I had said. Something that they must have heard countless times: 'Nearly all mothers,' the woman in charge told me with a wry smile, 'need to be reassured that they are doing the right thing before they leave their little ones with us – it's completely natural.'

I was introduced to a smiling nursery nurse who showed me around and took me to see a group of happy tiny tots. Some were already in what I thought of as a well-supervised play area, others were in baby chairs being spoon-fed puréed food. There was another room where the smallest babies of about Jade's age were being gently held and bottle-fed. Just watching those young women at work and seeing how even the tiniest ones reacted to them gave me the reassurance I needed and I knew my daughter would be well looked after here. She was used to a bottle because I had already started expressing milk so I handed over a Kool Bag and left her with the nurse. They were all so kind and promised to call me if there were any problems.

It felt so strange being without either child, but I had things to do and very little time left to enrol and commence Step Three. Back home, I looked through all the available courses and decided to complete my GCSEs. I was good at English, Maths, Biology and Geography so I decided to start there – if only there was a course on how to avoid a disastrous relationship, I would have signed up for that too.

By the end of the day when I collected a bathed, fed, rested and clean Jade, I knew the nursery was right for me if I was going to move forward with my plans. I sat down with the nursery supervisor and signed up for Jade to be there five days a week. Walking to the bus stop, I smiled down at my contented little one and rang Jean as I waited for the bus – 'I've done it, Jean! She's enrolled at the nursery. Tonight, I'll register for the first courses and start catching up on my studies.'

'Good for you, Ava!' she told me.

The only problem I had with taking my daughter to the nursery was that it was in the opposite direction to the school and so that meant I would need to travel on four buses a day. The price of a short bus ride might not sound expensive, but wait till you have to multiply it by twenty. Most of my meagre savings had gone into making the flat look like a home, so those fares would be coming out of my weekly allowance.

I would have to be more than frugal. Luckily, that was something I had learnt to be pretty good at while living with Dave – he was either flush with cash or stony broke and during the last couple of years, it was all too often the latter. Then I had learnt how to cook very cheap but healthy meals with just a few ingredients.

At least his gambling addiction had ensured that I had learnt one thing that would be useful now, I told myself. Shame that it had taken me so long to see through him though. I remembered then with a little wrench of my heart how excited he had been when I first told him I was pregnant and how he was over the moon when I gave birth to Justin. And now, not one penny would come from him to help feed and clothe our children. My solicitor had told me that because my former partner was unemployed, there was no chance of taking him to court. He might have been known to the police as a drug dealer, but they had never found enough on him for him to be charged.

But I knew if he wanted to send money he could, which made me feel pretty disgusted with him – not that that did me any good. Even with my child allowance and weekly benefits there was little left after I had bought food and paid our electricity bill. And growing children needed new clothes and shoes on a regular basis. Jean had told me she had some left over from when her children were younger but they were all pretty well worn out. They would be OK to play in, but I wouldn't want my son to look scruffy when he attended school – I had noticed that all the children I had seen in the playground looked pretty well turned out.

Later, I shared some of those thoughts with Jean, who came

round with a bottle of wine to celebrate my completion of Step Two and starting on the third step. She came up with an idea of how I could make some money, an idea that made me want to stuff my fingers in my ears so I couldn't hear what she had to say.

'Look, Ava, there's a club not far from here where you could work. They pay very well, so that could sort your money problems out,' she suggested in an almost casual way.

'What sort of club?'

'One where there're no questions asked about tax or anything like that. They pay in cash. You don't even have to give your right name. And let's face it, if you looked for a part-time job you would only be allowed to earn a tiny amount without it affecting your benefits.'

'Jean! Hang on there, are you suggesting I work in a brothel? Because this doesn't sound like a normal sort of club to me.'

'No, don't be silly, it's nothing like that. It's an exotic club, or a strip club if you like.'

'Not much difference to a brothel then, is it? No way could I bring myself to do that.'

But Jean just smiled and topped up our glasses. 'Come on, Ava, it would sort out all your money problems. The girls there make really good money,' she said encouragingly.

'No, forget it, no way!'

Not being someone who gave up easily, Jean then asked me how I thought students without well-off parents got themselves through uni these days.

'They have grants, don't they?' I said.

'Loans, more like it. Still, they're not so generous that students don't end up broke at the end of each month but there's all sorts of part-time jobs they take – I'm sure you've noticed them waitressing. Hard work, that, and not everyone tips. On top of it, they still have hours of studying to do. Then there are the ones who choose to earn what they see as easier money in clubs like the one near here. And let's face it, Ava, you've got a great body and it's that which will bring you in the cash. Before you say you can't leave your children at home alone, I'll come and babysit for you when you're working – as long as you bring back a bottle of wine, that is!'

'Look, I'm not going to do it, Jean – I'd feel like a prostitute.'

'Oh, don't be such a prude, Ava. Students don't seem to mind, nor do others who can't make ends meet easily. And you dance well too, which is all you have to do. Trust me, the men aren't even allowed to touch you.'

'So all I have to do is dance a bit?' I asked.

'That and taking your clothes off.'

'No way! I'm not dancing round in my birthday suit in front of a load of lecherous men.'

'Well, they're the losers, not you. They can drool all they like, but they're not allowed to move an inch towards you. Just hear me out for a minute or two before you turn your nose up again. The stage light goes off at the same time as the last bit of your clothing does, then you scuttle offstage and into a waiting robe. There's plenty of security there. No one's allowed to bother you before, during and after your dance. And you would be paid £20 for each of those fifteen minutes.

With your looks, you should get at least three or four sets and maybe more on a busy night. And sometimes the men tip too.'

I have to say the thought of pocketing around sixty quid in one night did register with me, as did her next comment: 'Over a weekend I've known a girl take away several hundred pounds. Trust me, the men aren't even allowed to touch you. Look, you don't have to do it forever, but you could stash a bit of money away as an emergency fund. Then you won't have to gasp with shock and swear each time the electricity bill comes in or when the monthly bill for using the internet arrives and you need that to study. Or even when Justin tells you that his shoes are hurting his toes or Jade has outgrown all her clothes.'

'So, how do you know all that anyway, Jean?' I said after a pause.

'You know, once he was gone, I never wanted to sleep in the main bedroom again. OK, I might have moved, but I still had to sleep in the same bed. So, I got rid of it, put in twin beds and rented it out to students. Had a couple of girls, nice ones who worked at the club. They told me all about it, took me out with them to a really posh restaurant once they made their first big amount. It got them through uni and now I can pass that bit of knowledge on to you.'

Finally, what Jean was saying was starting to sink in. After all, if I panicked at four bus fares a day, how was I going to manage the other things? So, in the end I agreed to give it a try.

Jean handed me the phone number scribbled on a piece of paper she had in her purse.

'Just ring it tomorrow, Ava,' she told me.

So, I did, though I just about stuttered with nerves when I made that call. All the voice at the other end of the line said was that there were some vacancies, but I needed to come for an interview first.

Meaning of course that he wanted to have a good look at me.

* * *

I had felt nervous quite a few times in my life, but not as much as I did when I reached the door to the strip club. *Did it have to be in the middle of a rundown but busy street?* I thought irritably. *I mean, just how many people doing their shopping would see me go in? Imagine if one of the mums I had met at the school or the crèche happened to be around.*

So what? my inner voice said. *Why would they know what was behind the door, even if their husbands did? Best get in quickly then*, it muttered again, *just pull your shoulders back and ring that bell.*

Screwing up my courage, I pressed the bell and then saw a tiny camera over my head move, telling the man inside that I had turned up for my appointment. My weaker self wanted to turn on my heels and run for the hills. But I had been told what to do over the phone and when I heard a click, I pushed the door open and headed downstairs, where Des would be waiting for me. My heart was pounding as I took the stairs to what I saw was a really gloomy basement – I suppose the dark red walls were meant to lend a sultry atmosphere. And with the lights on at night it might have achieved this, but the scant daylight showed what it really was – seedy. As was the portly man with his slicked-back, dark hair and bright beady eyes, which were already scanning up and down my body.

'I see you've got great legs,' he noted as I reached the bottom step.

Why had I worn a skirt? I wondered irritably. *Because Jean had told me to – I wonder why that was?!*

Beady-eyed or not, the man put his hand out to shake mine and then took me into his office.

'I can tell you've not worked in a place like this before, have you?' he said once I was seated.

Was he going to ask me to strip so he could check the rest of me out? I couldn't help but wonder what his next move would be.

'I know you're nervous but you don't need to be – all the girls are well looked after in here,' he told me with a reassuring smile. And then, instead of asking me to show him my body, he went over the house rules. How the 'punters', as he called them, were not allowed to come near us. Nor were we allowed to make plans to meet up with them outside the club.

'That's the only sackable offence,' he explained. If the girls thought they could make extra money by doing that, he could lose his licence – 'We're an entertainment club, not a dating agency or a pick-up place for men to get sex.'

After hearing him say that, I began to feel more at ease.

'And I see you have a toned body, so only one question, how's your dancing?'

'Not bad,' I muttered.

'Thought you would be good.'

He then explained how the money worked: there were small private rooms, 'VIP ones' was how he described them, 'where we pay you a straight twenty pounds to dance to just one song. But those are for small groups who often are celebrating something, like one of them is getting married the next day, or a big business deal. They usually tip a lot more than that.

'Any questions?' he added.

'No,' I gasped.

'Then I'll show you around,' he said nonchalantly as he turned on more lights in the club.

I suppose at night, the place would look a lot more sensuous. When Des showed me the individual rooms with their small stages, he pointed to where the hidden cameras were located – 'We need to make sure there's no monkey business going on. Security will be in there in a flash if they misbehave and all the punters know that.'

Seems as if that's the bonus for the security guys was the thought that jumped into my head, though I didn't say anything.

He then showed me the bar, with its gilded mirrors and prints of various scantily dressed, attractive women on the walls, which in its own way was quite glamorous. The last part of the club he showed me was the changing room, which was done up better than I had expected.

'The students bring their homework here, so the lighting has to be good for more than putting on make-up,' he told me with a grin. 'They work away between dances!'

Just when I was beginning to feel relaxed, Des showed me one of the costumes. Not much bigger than a high-cut strapless swimsuit, it was made of several pieces held together by press studs.

'The girls will show you what to do with them,' he explained. 'They come off in parts, then as the song finishes, the last part is dropped onto the floor and the lights go down, pronto!'

I felt my eyes widen when I saw what the last piece was. Until then, I had thought at least there would be three cutout pieces left, but no, there weren't. It meant that lights off or not, even the security guards would be watching me flashing my privates around.

'Oh, they only see you for a few seconds when that last bit comes off,' he said in such a matter-of-fact way. 'Just make sure you have a bikini wax the day before you arrive, if you haven't already.'

Boy, how I felt my cheeks burn at that. He, however, just saw it as a business necessity. He hadn't asked me any personal questions or made any objections or comments – well apart from 'nice legs' that is. He then showed me out, saying he would see me on Friday.

So, that was that – I was officially employed in a strip club!

21

I can't say I was looking forward to that first Friday night. In fact, my stomach was churning with nerves every time I thought about it.

'Imagine yourself dancing in your bedroom in front of the mirror,' Jean told me. 'Or that you're doing some kind of workout, and just look above the heads of those in front of you so you don't have to make eye contact. And if that doesn't work, just think of the £1.33 dropping into your purse as every minute slips by. Remember, they're not allowed to talk to you, far less lay a finger on your body, and each dance is over pretty quickly.'

'Yes, until the next one and the next one,' I said miserably.

But Jean took no notice and simply told me to pretend I was doing a nightly exercise routine to keep my body toned – her breeziness made me want to throw something straight at her!

'Thanks, Jean, I think I've got the message. So I'll lie away to myself all night then,' I said, sighing.

After I had tucked Jade into her cot, I kissed Justin good-night. He was sitting next to Jean on the settee and smiled contentedly up at me. With that, I picked up my bag and walked to the door. 'See you all later,' I said over my shoulder and then I drew my shoulders back to walk tall and set off.

I had been told to turn up at six, which was precisely the time I rang the doorbell.

A security guard opened the door to me – 'Ah, you're the new one Des told me about! Ava, isn't it?'

'Yes.'

'One of the girls is going to take you to the changing room, she's got your costume ready,' he told me with such a smirk on his face that I wished I could turn around and run back home. Instead, I gave him what I thought was a cool look – one that told him I didn't care what he thought and made my way down those stairs for the second time.

The petite brunette who was waiting for me was still dressed in her day clothes, a flowing flowery patterned skirt and a pale blue top. She introduced herself as Jo before telling me that as this was my first night, Des had asked her to keep an eye on me. I thought for a moment that she must have been his assistant but no, it soon became apparent that she was also working as a stripper, or as she called it 'an exotic dancer' when she took me to the changing room. I stopped myself from looking too surprised or saying, 'You hardly look like one.'

Which was just as well as I was about to learn that few of the dancers did.

With all the lights turned on, the changing room certainly had a different atmosphere than when I had seen it dimly lit. There were clothes strewn all over the place, the bulbs around the mirrors were all lit up, as a few scantily dressed women were touching up their make-up. No one took much notice of me as Jo took me over to one of the mirrors. She was to become someone I became really friendly with during the time I was there. It turned out her day job was teaching – 'Maths, can you believe?' she said, giving me a huge grin. 'I got through uni doing this and the day I heard I had a post at a good school, I never thought I would have to work here again.'

'So why are you back here then? A teacher's pay isn't that bad, is it?'

'No, that's nothing to do with it. I bought a flat with my fiancé and what a mistake that was! It was me who put the deposit down because I had my savings from here and he had nothing. Then he ditched me a week before the wedding. If that wasn't bad enough, him leaving could have made me lose the flat because it was in our joint names. Luckily, my parents helped out and we got it transferred into my sole name but now I have to manage the mortgage payments and bills all on my own. Can't take any more out of my parents' savings, they're not rich. So here I am again … Now I know you're new and bound to be feeling nervous. So, do what I recommend. Blank out your audience and just dance. It does get easier, you know, after the first few.'

She then showed me the costume and told me that once I had it on, she would help me with my make-up – 'It's not as though you look as if you need it, it's just that the stage lights drain all the colour from anyone's face.'

Tearing off my jeans and shirt, I blushed as I removed my underwear. I quickly grabbed my costume and wriggled into what looked a bit like a red corset, only instead of laces there were loads of press studs. Jo showed me how, as I danced, all my fingers had to do was flick these studs so that each piece of the costume would slide off my body easily.

Too easily, I thought sadly and I felt the blush rising again.

'Hey, you look great in that costume! Shows off those long legs of yours,' she told me, passing over a little gown to wear over the top until I was called in to dance. 'Now, let's get started on putting some colour on your face,' she added, opening up a box of stage make-up. 'Lean back and I'll show you. Red lips it's got be. As for those green eyes of yours, let's make them look even bigger. I can see you don't need false eyelashes, lucky you! Still, we'd better get plenty of mascara on them.'

Around twenty minutes later, with three coats of mascara on my lashes and all that stage make-up on my face, I glanced in the mirror and struggled to recognise myself. It also felt as sticky as anything!

Jo laughed when I told her that – 'The good thing about full stage make-up is that it's such a great camouflage. No one's going to recognise you outside in the daylight. Imagine if the Headmaster or one of the dads was in the audience! I really appreciate hiding behind this mask, I can tell you, Ava.'

Well, that observation alone was enough to make me happier to put up with a bit of stickiness.

I watched with intent fascination as Jo turned herself into a glamorous siren – 'Hate having to wear such high heels,' was her only complaint as she slipped into a black costume and skilfully applied her make-up.

What can I say about my first session, except that I was

shaking when I walked onto that stage. That first audience were made up of half a dozen fairly young men out on a stag party. The moment the stage light came on, so did the music – a fast-paced rendering of 'I Want to Love You'. *Did they have to put that on?* I thought as I let my limbs move to the rhythm.

The group were all pretty drunk and a bit rowdy, but to be fair, there were no unpleasant remarks. They just egged each other on to call out their appreciation, poured themselves more drinks, applauded loudly when the lights went off and I was to find out later that they had left me a pretty large tip.

On went my gown, as I trotted off as fast as I could in the darkness on my way to the changing room. The venue was certainly popular with stag parties, I soon found out.

I went home with nearly a hundred pounds. There was no feedback from Des – I would soon learn that as far as he was concerned, girls were just moneymaking machines. Apart from Jo being kind to me and the money, I had hated everything about my first night.

22

So, what can I tell you about the strip club? First, there was the clientele, who I would soon learn came from every walk of life. There were young and old, black, Asian and white, rich and poor … The one thing those men had in common was their desire to watch young women take their clothes off. Did they see the women there as people and ever wonder why they had to earn money that way? I don't think so; they just saw bodies they could talk about among themselves without any concerns about us hearing them. I hated being so sexualised.

Did they ever wonder what sort of women worked there? Had they asked me, I would have answered all sorts. And all of them worked there for different reasons. I knew some had the travelling bug and they would imagine themselves dancing on a beach in Bali or Thailand each time they performed. A group of students, who kept pretty much to themselves, studied diligently in between dances. There were a few single mums like myself, who just couldn't make ends meet, and several very pretty Eastern Europe girls who spoke little English. Seeing the number of dances they gave, I knew they earned good money.

I wondered what they did with it, for there was no sign of expensive new clothes or handbags. Even their lingerie was far from new and the questions that floated in my mind were how had they had come here and who had suggested they work in the club. At least they hadn't fallen into the hands of the gangs who sought them out. My first thought was that maybe they had linked up with the wrong men, the second was that they might have been sending as much of their earnings as they could back home, supporting their families abroad. But I would never find out the answers to these questions.

Then there were a couple of women working at the club who had no mystery whatever about them. Or any discretion, for that matter. One was a busty peroxide blonde and she shot glances at me before nudging her flame-haired friend as she pointed me out. One look at them told me they were best avoided. I had seen those types before, hardened bullies as children and bullies as adults. Seeing I was a new face, they didn't waste much time before they approached me. Their aim, I realised straight away, was to make me feel as uncountable as possible. They hardly drew breath as they started telling me smugly about their years stripping and how much they loved it.

'Gives me a real kick when the last piece of clothing hits the floor,' the brassy one told me with an unpleasant leery smile.

'Yeah, me too,' her red-haired friend sighed. 'Sure you're gonna feel the same soon enough, luv. Really turns us on, just looking down at those men's flushed faces. Makes us wriggle a bit more so it gets them all aroused, that does.'

'Yup, it's difficult not to laugh when we see their hands

wandering down to those little private parts of theirs,' said the brassy one and they both screamed with laughter at the thought. 'Can see you're new here, but don't you be shy. Have a go at doing the same and your tips will be better.'

I just managed to look blankly back at them.

'If you had better manners, you would be thanking us for being so helpful,' she added.

Thankfully, before I could utter a word, they sauntered off, sniggering.

'Those kinky ones are always boasting and they try and be intimidating by picking on newbies, that sort of thing. Try not to let them bother you, just avoid them,' Jo advised.

I was to do the same with a few others as well.

* * *

Every night when I worked at the club, I was so relieved when I had finished my last dance at midnight (the time I had stated that I needed to leave by) – all I wanted was to go home and have a drink with Jean before falling into bed. But I had one more thing to go through: the gauntlet of the sleazy security guards, who managed to let us know they had been watching those cameras a little too intently.

As I said, I hated my first night and I hated my last one too, a few months later. But I can't say I hated anything about my earnings. They certainly made a difference to my life. I was able to squirrel most of that money away for my 'emergency fund' as Jean had called it. And with that in place, I now felt that my little family was more secure.

It was Jean who, one evening when I returned from the club, gave me the advice I had to accept was needed. As we shared the last of the bottle of red wine she looked me in the eyes and said she felt that I was strong enough to move on to the next phase of my emotional life. Having benefited from years of counselling, she was now considering training as a therapist herself. She convinced me that I needed to take myself back to my early childhood years and try to work out just what went wrong – 'Because let's face it, Ava, nothing just happens overnight, does it? I really believe the mistakes we make in our adult life are often because of deeply embedded memories from our childhood. And there's a reason you never ever talk about yours. I know it's in your mind; I'm sure you lie in bed and ask yourself just how you ended up in a refuge with a highly disturbed child and a baby who could have died at the hands of your partner. And you need to find the answers to that. My advice is, just jump in that time machine and do it!'

Jean was right, of course: it was time I worked at unpacking all my past, right back from the beginning. Not just for my sake, but for my children's as well – they were bound to ask questions later on and I had better have the right answers ready.

She had made a point well and so I went to bed mulling over my childhood. For isn't it our early years that forms our characters? I could just tell you that mine was a bit messed-up, but that's not good enough, is it? I need to look with fresh eyes at all the things that destroyed my confidence before I had even turned fifteen. So, now is the time for me to look for the truth and find resolution in what happened.

Here goes …

23

Before I talk about my younger self, I need to focus a little on the two people who tried to shape me. Because from when I was very little, both my mother and the man I thought of as my dad did their best to plant their beliefs into my head. Not that I understood what they were straight away, for it takes a bit of maturity to start evaluating the opinions of others for oneself. It was when they started to become crystal clear to me that I began to feel I was no longer part of my own family. Going back to that time is still painful, but as they were the main presence in a large chunk of my early life, I can't avoid forcing myself to remember those years that I spent with them.

So, what were they like? To be fair, my mum was not afraid of hard work. Any job would do, from cleaning offices to being a lollipop lady. She had two reasons for working so hard to bring extra money into the home; one being that she was able to keep up her image of being a well-dressed and well-groomed woman, which to her was all-important. The second reason was so that she could add to their saving up for the future she was so determined to have. Her dream was to move up a little in the world, an ambition she made certain that her husband Ed shared with her. Although that should be something to admire, not criticise, because moving into a more spacious house in a better area should have benefited us all. Not that I can remember much about my first home. Just that it was rather a small flat, though I do have quite a clear memory of moving into a large 1970s house when I was five, most probably because I was so delighted to find that I was getting a bedroom all to myself instead of sharing with my baby sister.

Now that Mum had finally succeeded in the first step of moving up in the world, she became even more fussy about her appearance. So, what did she look like? Now for those of you who remember singer Rod Stewart in the days when he wore tighter-than-tight jeans, you might be able to picture his hairstyle: short and spiky on top, long at the sides, loads of blond streaks. It seemed all the women in my mother's circle copied it. Well, she certainly did and it was to remain her hairstyle over all the years I knew her. I have to say, looking back at my childhood, she did seem to be stuck in the eighties styles and as for the man I called Dad, he was, as I was to discover, stuck a little further back in time, albeit for very different reasons – but I'll come to what that means a little later on.

If I close my eyes and concentrate a little, I can picture my mother now. Neither unduly tall nor short, she was a well-rounded woman who never left the house without her bright blue eyeliner, bold coloured clothes with huge shoulder pads, feet tucked into shiny stilettos and enormous sunglasses perched on her nose or if it became dusk, on the top of her head among the gelled spikes of hair. Inside the house she was just as meticulous – not one item was ever allowed to be out of place, every room had to look as immaculate as she did. Should visitors be expected or she had to take me with her when she went shopping, she made sure that I too looked smart. No casual kids' outfits for me. Instead, over my head went one of my dresses with puffy short sleeves, up went my hair into a neat ponytail and my small feet were thrust into white socks before a pair of Clarks leather patent shoes were pushed onto them.

All of this was a bit difficult for a five-year-old who liked playing in the garden. All too often my mum would get annoyed when I appeared with dirt on my hand and knees, my hair in a mess. I can't say she was an unkind mother, just a very strict one. God help me if I got dirt on my clothes, scuffed my shoes or left any of my toys lying around just before visitors arrived. But that didn't stop me from loving her and wanting her attention. I can remember all the different ways I tried to get it – 'What is it you want now, Ava?' was her exasperated response almost every time I called out the word 'Mum' and that response which made any words I wanted to say dry up. Attention, warm smiles and cuddles were just not her thing. Nor was she a mother who read me stories or thought of games to play with me.

Luckily for my formative years, I was unaware that this was what loving mothers often did. They also tucked their children into bed and kissed them goodnight, something else that was missing during my early years. Once she had helped me get undressed and hung my clothes up in the wardrobe, she made sure the light was turned off as soon as I was in my night clothes before she marched down the stairs. Then I really couldn't understand what was lacking in our relationship, far less what the reason might have been. But by the time I reached ten, I did.

My memories of the man I called 'Dad' are a little different from the ones I have of my mother. Talk about complete opposites when it came to their dress codes. Fashion was not something he was interested in. Instead in summer, it was T-shirts and jeans, then in winter a leather jacket was added. And what did he look like? Well, he was tall and muscular, with a totally shaven head. He rode a powerful and noisy motorbike, as did most of his friends. Our neighbours looked on with disapproval as they roared down the road to visit him. I suppose he must have looked a bit hard, even unapproachable, but in those early years, to me he was always friendly and kind. He was someone who I liked trotting behind because a smile would light up his face whenever he glanced down at me, before one of his large tattooed hands gave my head a comforting pat.

24

So, what happened to make me begin to see what was wrong in my life? I suppose it started when my baby sister arrived in the world. I had been told quite a while earlier that Mum was going away for a few days and when she returned home, she would be bringing back my baby sister or brother. What I can't remember was who it was who told me, either my mum or Mum's sister Betty, who I was sent to stay with for a few days. I should think it was her. She had a home that I enjoyed being in – off would come my pristine clean dress and on would go a pair of one of my cousins' old shorts and a bright top of some kind. She never minded if we kids got ourselves dirty when we were outside in the large rubber paddling pool or playing hide-and-seek in the bushes. In fact, she rarely ticked any of us off and the house was full of toys and laughter. When we messed ourselves up, hot baths were run and the washing machine was loaded with our grubby clothes.

It was my aunt who told me that I had a baby sister and promised that I would be meeting her very soon. 'She's going to be called Dawn,' she said, not adding that my mother had decided on that name because she gave birth just as the sun was rising. Hearing that I now had a sibling made me feel excited – I might have someone to play with was my immediate thought. I could hardly wait to see her. It was a few days later when my aunt took me back to my home and there was my mother sitting on the settee, with my baby sister, Dawn, all wrapped in pink, cuddled in her arms. Looking at my mother, I was surprised to see her adoring expression as she studied the baby. It was an emotion I had never seen on her face before.

For the first few months, when I saw my baby sister cooed to and cuddled, did I really think all that attention was because she was a baby? Or did I begin to feel that my sister was loved more than me? I know I tried to get some affection for myself by moving closer and leaning against my mother's legs. That didn't work and instead I heard her muttering, 'Oh, for goodness' sake, Ava, stand up straight or go and sit down somewhere else,' as she pushed me firmly away.

I suppose that was the beginning of me feeling unloved.

As Dawn grew and started crawling and then taking little tottering steps, I would watch my mother showing her pictures in the assortment of children's books that had appeared in our house and chanting nursery rhymes to her. Not that my sister could repeat one word, but she managed baby chuckles, which put a proud smile on Mum's face.

Even then I believed, maybe because I wanted to, that she must have given me the same attention when I was little. Not that I had any recollection of her doing so, although that was something I stopped telling myself when I was five and my sister nearly three. An incident in the garden made me see just how much love my mother had for Dawn – it was in her voice, her face, even her body. It was just that none of that love was ever directed towards me.

So, what happened on that day?

My sister was little more than a toddler when the accident happened. Even then she was the most determined, or should I say wilful little girl I have ever met, though with her blonde curls and big blue eyes, she had the face of an innocent cherub. Well, looks can be deceptive, can't they? It was not long after we had moved that Mum told me to get out from under her feet and go outside and play so off I went, with Dawn following me. Even though her talk was a babble of indistinguishable words I picked up a couple – 'go fishing'. Goodness knows where that came from, perhaps it was in one of the stories Mum read to her.

With that devilish grin of hers, she clutched the handle of a small broom that had been left outside and dragged it over to the centre of the garden, where the fish pond was. Once there, she gave another grin as she sat herself down and began stirring up the water with the broom. It was a good thing that the previous owners had taken their fish with them or they would hardly have been happy being poked about by a brush. Now at five I didn't see any danger in playing there, I just thought we were having fun as I dragged over a mop that was drying by the back door and then giggling away with Dawn, I too pretended to fish.

At that age we were just two little girls living in the pictures that imagination can place in their minds. I was so busy pretending that the imaginary fish were nibbling at the strands of the mop and talking away to them that for a few seconds I hadn't noticed what Dawn was up to. She had decided to sit on the edge of the pond so she could dangle her legs in the water and just when I was looking up at her, she leant too far over and fell face down in the pond. The moment I heard the splash I screamed as loud as I could for Mum to come, while at the same time I jumped in and grabbed hold of my sister. I wasn't that strong, but I still managed to get her head above the water so she could catch some air.

Mum came rushing out. By that time Dawn had enough air in her lungs to bellow out her rage at having fallen in. At which point my dad and his friend, who was helping with some repairs upstairs, came running out in a complete panic.

The two men blamed themselves for not having the pond covered, while Mum, without saying a word, carried my screaming sister into the house. For the rest of the afternoon Dawn was sat on Mum's knee, being fed treats and cuddled, while I sat near the window watching as Dad and his friend used buckets to empty the pond of its water.

Mum was quite hysterical about the accident. She kept repeating that Dawn could have drowned. And yes, she might have done, had I not been there to lift her head out of the water. And really, what I succeeded in doing by grabbing her and pulling her head up so she could breathe was actually quite a big thing for a five-year-old to manage. Not that anyone ever mentioned it, they didn't even ask if I was all right: all the attention was on my sister and I was just ignored.

Did I become bitter and jealous from that time? No, not really, it was more that I felt sad and lonely. But I can't say that my mother's lack of feelings towards me doesn't still hurt almost as much today as then. There are times when I look in the mirror and see not me, but the ghost of my younger self: a little girl with crimped hair and pink bows in her bunches, wearing a frilly dress that she has been told not to get dirty. She's only around five but I can tell by the expression in her eyes that she is already feeling unwanted.

Oh, my younger self was always well fed, was dressed in nice clothes and always received thoughtful presents on birthdays and at Christmas. That was my mother's duty and as I have said, she made sure she did what was expected, but never any more.

25

I was ten when a really major piece of knowledge, flung almost carelessly in my direction, just about knocked me sideways. I can remember every detail of that day when I was told a story I was too young to really understand. And who was it who decided that I should know all of it? It was the man I believed was my dad.

If Ed hadn't been drinking since lunchtime, maybe he would have waited a couple of years before telling me what had taken place before I was born. Surely the correct way of telling a child the truth about who they are should be done as tactfully as possible by both their parents. I might not have felt so traumatised if I hadn't had to listen to just one of them spilling the beans when he was far from sober. Not that being worse for wear at the weekends was unusual for my parents. I've not mentioned before that both of them were heavy drinkers, have I? Well, they really were. It was their way of relaxing after working hard all week. And often they invited equally boozy friends over for dinner.

Of course, I was sent to bed just about the same time as

they were tottering around, filling up their glasses for the third or fourth time though sometimes they seemed to forget I was there. Still, I was only too happy to slide quickly out of the door and make my escape. I suppose seeing them pour liquid out of bottles that were not for children had been so much part of my early years that I hadn't really given it much thought. But by the time I was ten I had worked out just how much alcohol can change adults' moods and I have to say it was seldom for the better.

On that afternoon, Mum had already staggered off to bed for 'an afternoon nap', as she called it and I was left alone with the man I called Dad. My little sister was spending the day with our aunt as it was our cousin's sixth birthday party, not one I had wanted to go to.

Later that day, I really wished I had.

It was when the man that I thought of as Dad poured himself yet another drink and filled a large beer glass with cola for me – strange as I was not usually allowed to drink it – that I felt something was about to happen. Still, at least he hadn't been drunk enough to also pour some brandy into it as I'd seen him do for his friends.

As he handed it to me I received a penetrating look before he said, 'You know, Ava, there's something I think you need to know,' a statement that made me feel even more uncomfortable. I had this unnerving feeling that I was about to be told something I wouldn't want to hear. Maybe it was because his voice was really slurring that my apprehension became even more intense. Sober, he was pretty quiet, but drink changed him and made him more talkative. And a lot of what I heard him and his friends saying made me squirm with embarrassment. Sentiments like 'Those bloody P*kis should go home,' were expressions I had already come to hate. After all, nearly half the pupils in my school came from different countries around the world or rather, their parents did, and I had made friends with quite a few of them. Although even at ten, I had known enough about their prejudices not to mention this to my parents.

I was too young then to realise that the man I called Dad was a racist. Though that was not a word I had learnt the true meaning of yet. But I had seen him switching the radio off when soul music came on – 'Not listing to that jungle bunny stuff,' I had heard him say more than once. And if Trevor McDonald was presenting the news on TV, off it would go. As for black actors on TV, just the sight of one in a film or series would make him turn the television off or find another channel to watch. Then there were series like *Dallas* and *Dynasty* that were my mum's favourites although both of them watched. She loved what she saw as all the glamour in them. Well, that was over twenty years ago and I'd hate to think what a problem it must be for him now. So that day I was wondering if he had caught sight of me walking home from school with some of my friends and wanted to talk to me about it – not that I really understood his reasoning, not then anyway.

His voice broke into my thoughts as he said, 'Come on, Ava, there's a nice breeze outside, we can talk out there,' and although I would have liked to disappear into my room I had no choice but to follow him into the long, well-kept garden.

Gardening was about Mum's only hobby and she certainly had done a good job in making it attractive. Not that I was paying much attention to flowering borders that day, I was too worried about what my father wanted to discuss. We ended up sitting on two of the sun loungers and all I can remember about his opening conversation was that he wanted me to know that he had loved me ever since I was a baby. I have to say this was a pretty unusual and sentimental speech from him, though hearing him say it made me feel warm inside. Especially when he added that the moment he had seen me, he had believed that I was going to be a special child. Not that his next sentence had the same effect – it just about floored me, in fact.

'Ava, I think you're old enough to know the truth: I'm not your real dad. I just felt the time was right to tell you that.'

For a moment I thought this must be some kind of weird joke. Or maybe some sort of test to see what I would say, so I stayed quiet, waiting to hear what he would say next. But it appeared that it wasn't the joke I was hoping it was. He took another large swallow of his drink and then began telling me all about my real dad – 'You look like him, Ava. You have the same green eyes and not many people have them, do they? Both of you have that sort of pale bronze hair and now you're growing, it looks like you're going to be tall like him as well. I think that's something your mother finds difficult – not that it's your fault, of course.'

That's good to know, I thought to myself crossly as in my mind I tried to picture the father I had never known I had.

If that wasn't enough to shock me, I was then told that I

had two older brothers who were still living with their father. Well, I suppose to be absolutely correct, they were living with *my* father too, I wanted to say.

'So, what other relatives do I have out there?' I asked him breathlessly.

'A stepmother and another aunt, don't know about the rest. Mind you, I hear that woman your father married is a right bitch and as for your dad ... well, Ava, you've been better off with me. Your mum hasn't a good word to say about him. Trust me, he's not that nice.'

Mum had certainly kept all of this very quiet. I had never even heard a hint of it, not from her, my aunt or anyone else for that matter.

'So why hasn't Mum told me herself?' I asked him.

'Not something she likes to talk about,' was hardly an answer that satisfied me. Even worse, in a way probably the worst part, was that I had never known that I was part of a larger family. Even if Mum didn't like my father, what about my older brothers? Why had I never known about them? And why did they not visit Mum – after all, she was their mum? These were just some of the questions I began to fire at the man I now knew to be my stepdad. Which was when he told me the rest of the story. Evidently my mum and my biological father had not been getting on for quite a while. It was during that time that she had met Ed and according to him, it hadn't taken her long to decide she would rather have a life with him than stay with her husband.

Of course that made me ask why. The answer was that my real dad was 'a bloody narcissist'. And if I didn't understand that word, he explained that it meant he was a man who felt so important that he expected his wife to hang on to his every word – 'He was a control freak from hell,' he added when he saw the puzzled look on my face.

Mind you, that might have described Mum as well, but somehow I managed to keep my mouth shut.

'Now your mum and I were waiting for the right time for her to make the break from him when unfortunately, she found out she was pregnant, just a few days after we made our decision. Your mum, thinking of morning sickness and doctor's appointments, just didn't feel it was the right time to go, so we delayed it for a while.'

That was when I worked out that it was me who had stood in the way of her living the life she wanted. Although other questions were firing up in my head, I waited for him to continue.

'She stayed with him until you were a few months old and then, not being able to stand your father for a moment longer, she rang me up and said she was leaving. Basically, she left the house with a couple of suitcases and you.'

'And my brothers?'

'She left them behind but she could hardly have left you with them when you were so little.'

'How old were they when she left them?'

'Seven and four, but don't look so worried, she had called on someone to babysit until he got home from work. She left him a letter as well.'

The thought that entered my head then, and in reality, has never left it, was that she must have been pretty fed up at not being able to leave me behind too. After all, I could hardly have been a baby she wanted to have. Which I suppose was one of the reasons she really did not like me. In a way hearing all this came as a bit of relief. Ever since I was five I had wondered what I had done wrong. The answer to that was the only thing I was guilty of: being born. It made me completely downcast and I now know that I was just too young and naive to take it all in. Of course I felt sad, I wanted to run to my room and cry. No matter what my stepfather Ed had said about loving me, he loved Dawn far more. Both of them looked so proud of her, for she was the child that they had always wanted.

So that was the day when everything made sense. Mum was never proud of me, no matter how well I swam for my club, or how good my school reports were. Nor did she seem pleased when I completed my household chores. The saddest thing really was that I loved both my stepfather and my mum with all my heart. In a way I still do. Not that I think I will ever see them again, nor will my beautiful children ever meet their grandparents.

One day I will have to explain to them why that is and I just pray that learning the reason will not damage them as well. For neither my stepfather nor my mother would ever acknowledge who they were. I doubt now if they will ever want to see me again. As for their grandchildren, they will never want to acknowledge them.

26

Up until the time Ed told me that he was not my father, I had never questioned whether we were an ordinary family or not. To the outside world I'm sure we must have looked as though we were. Well, as much as a middle-aged skinhead and a woman with thick blue eyeliner and a Rod Stewart hairstyle would. But inside our four walls, I didn't consider we really were a family. Had they not, for whatever reason, bought their house in Leicester, maybe I still wouldn't have so many questions about them running through my head.

Why, I ask myself now, did a couple with their views, decide to live in a town where over fifty per cent of the people were, as they referred to them, 'non-white'? And that's just one of the many questions I will never know the answer to.

* * *

The next memory I have, which follows shortly after Ed told me he was not my father, was when he sat me down and spelt out to me who would be welcome in his house; or rather, who wouldn't be. Up until then I had seen him as a man who seldom became angry and was always kind to me, but that day I began to see a rather different side of him. It might have been his hatred of other races and cultures that had made him bitter, but for me, hearing some of his beliefs certainly made me feel extremely uneasy. Oh, he tried his best not to let me see exactly how deep his feelings were, he was too smart to spill everything out in one go. But children can sense, I suspect, far more than adults give them credit for – just what some terms mean. In my case I knew he was trying to make me share his opinions. He must have believed that if he let me know them in stages, I would gradually go along with him and adopt them as my own.

Looking back, my stepdad must have been living in the past when gangs of skinheads led protest marches from the seventies to the nineties to show their resentment of immigrants coming into the UK. Marches, I later learnt, that led to unspeakable violence. But it seemed he had no idea that I was a student in the twenty-first century, where a new generation of teachers did their utmost to encourage children of different cultures to mix and appreciate each other's beliefs and values.

Had he had stood looking into my school's playground at break times, he would have seen children of all different shades playing together. And if he had been there at the beginning of the day, when mums arrived with their kids, he would have noticed that they too were chatting easily with each other. As older children walked to school or got off the bus together, they too seemed oblivious to racial divides. My stepfather had no understanding that children of eleven are unlikely to be persuaded not to make friends with children from different backgrounds. Not when they have been at school with them since they were five. Maybe he should have aired his views a little earlier, but he didn't. Instead he waited until I was in my last term at junior school to try and make me share his views. As he spoke, I could understand his words, but not the reasoning behind them.

The main one being, had I any sense, I would not make black or brown children my friends.

'Look, Ava, they might seem all right, but I've been around a lot longer than you and I know they're not to be trusted. Now in a couple of months you are off to senior school, where it's important to begin making good friends so please make them white ones. Best if we mix with each other and let those others mix with themselves.'

That was his take on trying to be tactful!

What my stepdad did not realise was that during the five years I had been at my school, no one was judged because of their colour. They might be judged for other reasons, like sticky-out ears, being fat or thin or having ginger hair, but that was about all. So, the more he spoke, the more confused I became. Not only confused but embarrassed as well. He, on the other hand, must have believed that the more he spouted out his racist views, the more I would begin to share them. Over the next four years that I stayed with him, he never understood that he had told me all this much too late – if you want to brainwash a child, then do so before they have formed any of their own beliefs.

Now I'm not that naive that I don't know that many young

people modify their early views as they mature. Newspaper headlines have told us about cases using words like 'climate activist', 'radicalised' and 'extremist'.

All I can say is that my stepfather had no success with me.

27

The first term at my senior school was not that easy for me at the beginning. I had gone from being a senior in my first school to a junior in the high school. That was quite a big eye-opener for instead of being used to the little ones looking up to us, we were now made to feel like tiny minnows in a sea full of sharks!

So, am I saying there was bullying in the school? Yes, I am. Which made it important in our first year there to give the right impression. Appearing to be a bit of a doormat was definitely out. Chin up, shoulders back and walk with confidence was what I told myself. That worked and by the end of my first term I was pretty popular, which made me happy. I mean, that was what school was all about, wasn't it? Hadn't my parents said that was when we made the friends who would still be in our lives when we were adults? And they had also drummed into me that getting good grades was important if I wanted a decent job in the future. They had also told me in no uncertain terms that the friends I made should be white. That bit of unpleasant advice was something I pushed to the back of my mind.

Unfortunately for me, my parents had not done likewise.

I realised pretty quickly though that I had reached the age when my parents believed that searching questions were necessary if I didn't come straight home from school. As we were all that little bit older, we received a lot more homework. Visiting each other in our homes and working on some subjects together had become fairly usual, or at least I could say it was a good excuse not to go straight home, anyhow. Then when the weekends were just around the corner it was normal to make plans to meet up. Though even if they hadn't been, if someone woke up to a sunny day, often they called round to a friend's house to see what they were up to.

It was one of those impulsive visits that caused me more problems at home. Just how embarrassing was it the first time when a couple of girls called round to see if I wanted to go to the park with them? At least that's what they told me later as Mum didn't give them time to say why they were there – she just snapped that I was busy before slamming the door in their faces.

'You have homework to do, Ava,' was the first excuse she made for her rudeness.

The second time another girl called on me and got the same reaction, Mum told me the truth – at least *her* truth: 'You've got to stop them coming round here, Ava. And you certainly can't let them in – your dad won't have them in the house. He doesn't want them ringing his doorbell either, what will the neighbours think? So, if I'm out and you answer the door, I don't care what excuse you make so long as they don't put a foot inside. Say you're helping me with chores or something like that – which, if you're not careful, I can make sure you spend all your free time doing. You know if you would just listen to our opinions instead of ignoring them, your life might be easier. From what I've seen, you're very indiscriminate about who you have as friends and let me tell you, unless you wise up a bit, it's going to cause you a lot of trouble.'

'But over half my class isn't white, Mum,' I protested.

'Then make friends with the other half, Ava – that's all your dad and I want. Do you understand me?'

'Yes.'

Of course, I got what she meant, as did my friends who had experienced her rudeness when they called round. They must have found her attitude very hurtful and they would have known straight away what it was all about.

As an adult, I have come across some people who are not that happy about the migrant families who have settled here but I've never met one who would make a well-turned-out, polite little girl of eleven feel inferior because she wasn't white. My mother was so keen to support my stepdad's views that she gave no thought to the trouble her rudeness might have given me at school. I was lucky those girls had been kind enough not to get angry or run me down at school for if they had, my popularity would have gone out of the window. But they just said they knew it wasn't my fault and assured me we were still friends.

Mum must have thought I had made our house rules clear to the girls who had called round, or that she had, because after that, I had no more visitors. I partly made sure of that by saying my mother was very strict and expected me to spend time with my sister at weekends. What I was unaware of then was that my stepfather had ways of checking up on me. He had seen me in the playground, smiling and chatting with my classmates. Then I had to listen to both my parents making snide remarks about how all those immigrant children were wrecking the education system. The one thing they couldn't do was forbid me from speaking to them – not during school hours anyway. Surely they must have known what the school would do if I was reported for being racist? They would call in my parents, which ironically would be the last thing they would want.

It took me a couple more years to realise just how deep my stepdad's feelings about people from other countries who had settled in the UK were. Had I done so, I definitely would have lied about the party I was invited to. That's another memory that has not left my mind for it was the beginning of my relationship with my stepfather completely breaking down.

It began on a Friday, just as we were scrambling to get out of the classroom, when one of the girls I was friendly with came over.

'Hi, Ava, what are you doing on Saturday afternoon?'

In fact, I had been thinking of going round to my aunt's house to spend some time with my cousins. Saturday afternoons at home were when drinks were poured out, one after the other. I had little desire to spend time watching my parents knock them back and then complain about us having black sports commentators and newsreaders. As I thought Liyana might be suggesting something more interesting, I just told her that I had nothing really planned, except for doing my home-work and helping Mum with a few chores.

'That doesn't sound much fun, so would you like to come to my birthday party instead?'

Would I? Of course I would – anything to get away from home.

So, the answer was yes, which was not the same as my mother's when I was foolish enough to tell her that I had been invited to my classmate's birthday party. I couldn't have been thinking when I told her that, although I did say that quite a few from my class would be going.

'And what's your friend's name?' Mum asked.

Before I answered, I just knew what she was going to say. Had I been a little older, I might have thought of saying 'Susan' or 'Jane' or something like that, but no, I told her the right one.

'So she's a P*ki, is she?'

'Oh, come on, Mum! She was born here, she's British.'

'Don't ever let your dad hear you saying that. Doesn't matter where she was born, she's one of them. You should have known better than to think you could go and then you wouldn't even have bothered me by asking.'

Not that I had thought I was asking, I was just telling her about the invite.

'You should know by now how your dad feels, or are you just trying to make him angry?'

I could feel tears welling up – it was the first party I had been invited to in my new school and I wanted to go so much.

'Anyhow, the answer is no, you're not going. Now do you have her number?'

I felt like saying no, but it was on the address she had given me. Reluctantly, I said yes.

'Well, ring her now and make an excuse.'

Which I did, but I felt pretty unconvincing when I said it was because we had visitors coming that I had to stay in.

Liyana sounded more disappointed than suspicious. To my relief, she was as friendly as ever on the Monday morning when we were back at school. She told me all about the party and seemed really sorry that I hadn't been able to come.

'And I was disappointed as well,' I told her sincerely. 'No fun sitting around with Mum's relatives.'

Telling my mother about the invite was my first big mistake, one I was determined not to repeat. When I was next invited to a friend's house, I made sure both she and Ed believed she was white. Not that it made me feel good – in fact, it was just the opposite. I felt truly ashamed of being disloyal to my friends but in the end, if anything, it was my family I felt ashamed of more than I did of myself.

28

I did wonder a little what was said to my sister. I know from what Mum said to me much later, she had been worried I was going to be a bad influence on her. Which might be the reason why I saw so little of Dawn. At weekends, she went to Aunt Joan's house to play with my younger cousins. Being three years younger than me, she was already tucked up in bed while I was finishing off my homework. But I almost suspected that she had been told to keep out of my way. Something else I will never know for sure.

I was now always on my guard at home. When I told my mother I was going to Alice's house after school one Friday, I knew even though she had met her once at my swimming classes, she would still fire as many questions as she could think of before I left the house. Questions such as, is it just you or a group of your classmates who are going to be there? Doubtless she was worried that Alice's mother must be one of those liberals who didn't mind who came into her home.

'Oh no, Mum, it's just us and her family. She's going to help me with my homework,' I insisted.

Now that got me her immediate permission to go!

What really didn't work for me was when Mum took her turn in giving me similar lectures to the ones Ed had given me. All about how schooling was important and making the right friends and so on. She usually ended with words of wisdom such as 'that's why we have to be selective about who we choose to socialise with'. She encouraged me in my swimming lessons and suggested I enrol in some dancing ones as well. The coach had told me I was on track to race competitively as a swimmer and as for my first and last dance lesson, yes, I loved music – reggae, soul and hip hop – so shall I just say that I was the wrong daughter to learn the tango, waltz and foxtrot. The only good thing was that none of my classmates turned up to watch!

I just wished Mum hadn't turned up at one of those swimming coaching sessions. Instead of watching the speed of my breaststroke, she was more interested in which students I knew there. The moment she saw a couple of white ones coming in our direction she would ask if they were at my school. A few were, which made her face light up when we greeted each other.

I nearly died of embarrassment when two of my other schoolmates came over to praise my swimming. 'Bloody people!' Mum muttered when they walked away, having been completely snubbed by her – I just prayed that no one had overheard her even though she did little to modulate her volume. I did screw up my courage though and pointed out to her that they were in my year and we got on really well.

'Just make sure you try and sit next to a white one, Ava.

Bet those two stink of curry, probably their uniforms do too!'
she said with a sniff, as if the smell of biriyani was lingering
in the air.

Good idea, Mum, I thought. *I'd love to see my teacher's
face if I ever suggested that we change our seating because of
your and Ed's racism.*

Thankfully, she began to make excuses not to come with me
– she found it boring – so at least I was free to chat with whoever I wanted to. However, she would come to collect me and
looked more than annoyed when she saw me waving goodbye
to one of my not-white classmates. I don't think my parents
even acknowledged that I was working as hard as I could at
school – I wanted good grades and I wanted them to see that I
was doing well at school. Looking back, I can understand just
why that was. Then I was really desperate to hear some words
of praise coming from them, maybe even get a hug as I heard
them say, 'Oh, well done, darling, we're so proud of you.'

Well, that didn't happen; it never had done. It was not my
marks they were interested in, but who I was mixing with. By
the time I was twelve I realised that no matter what I did to
help around the house and however good my school grades
were, it made no difference to the fact that they did not trust
me to have the right friends. Since my first term at my senior
school, my stepdad had withdrawn much of his earlier friendliness. If that wasn't hurtful enough, my mother's distancing
herself from me certainly was. And still being of an age when
we are eager for our mother's affection, I was beginning to
feel isolated and lonely in my own home. If I hadn't faced up
to the fact by now that she didn't really like me, I had to then.

I might have worked out why that was and tried to put it to the back of my mind, but good old alcohol managed to bring it right to the fore.

When I heard the splash of booze being poured into glasses and the clink of ice cubes, I always wanted to make my escape. 'Better get on with my homework,' or something like that usually worked. But not if we were all watching something on television. I disliked seeing them drink and there would be Mum, staggering around in those high heels of hers, while she poured yet another couple of doubles. Ones that seemed to coat her tongue with pure venom. It was the third glass that usually released her from having to hide her feelings towards me. When I saw it being poured, I all but sighed as all I had to do was wait for those remarks she kept repeating to be aimed in my direction – one of the most charming being 'When I look at you, it's your dad I see. The more you grow, the more you look like him. You've got his colouring and his eyes and now it seems you're getting his character as well.'

After what my stepfather had told me about him, this was hardly a compliment. Not that I was expecting any – I just sat silently waiting for the next remarks, which I knew off by heart. Words such as 'control freak' and 'a cunning narcissist' who had stopped her seeing her lovely sons would be spat out.

'Bastard!' was about all my stepfather chipped in. A word that made Mum smile lovingly at him.

'Yes, he really is.'

No, I didn't like wet Saturday afternoons. And while I don't mind the odd glass of wine or two in the evening, I still cringe at daytime drinking.

29

There were two events which happened in the time when I was between the ages of eleven and thirteen; they were to be responsible for the biggest changes I was to face in my childhood. Not that at the time I had any idea of how my life was going to take another route, one that I should never have walked down.

The first one was when I met my younger brother Jonny. Something I had wanted to do ever since my stepdad had told me not only was he not my real dad, but that I had two brothers. I had asked Ed more than once when I was going to meet them. To begin with, he told me he didn't know, but it was when I asked him for about the third or fourth time that he became irritated – 'Oh, just forget about them. Your mother's ex has never shown any interest in you, has he? Not even a Christmas or birthday present or a card has come through the post for you, now has it?'

'No.'

'Well then, Ava, you should have worked it out for yourself.

Your biological dad doesn't want anything to do with you and I should think that your brothers have forgotten that you even exist so it's best you just try and forget about them. And stop asking me, OK?'

My answer to that was a reluctant 'yes'. But although probably true, I didn't want to believe what he had said and I couldn't stop thinking about them. Being a child with a degree of curiosity, whatever my stepdad told me, I really wished I could meet up with the other part of my family. Anyhow, didn't I look like them? That's what my stepdad had told me, wasn't it? He said it was my resemblance to my real dad that made Mum seem abrupt with me. Now that was a bit of an understatement – the excuse that she didn't want to be constantly reminded of her ex-husband didn't really work for me.

Ever since I had been filled in a little about my birth, I had thought her attitude towards me was more because having me had delayed her running off with Ed. I suppose underneath I was wishing for a family who I could feel I really belonged to and who actually wanted me in their lives. I couldn't help but fantasise about meeting up with them. Maybe Ed had got it wrong and my dad and brothers did want to see me. In my imagination I could almost see them arriving at our door, exclaiming they could hardly believe how alike we all were. That was a dream which lasted for a while and then as dreams do, it gradually faded away.

*   *   *

It must have been about a year after I had been told about my brothers that I met one of them, though how it was arranged was hardly normal. But then the one who set it up, my stepfather's sister Jeanette, was known for being a bit dozy. What she had never mentioned to Mum was that Jonny, my younger brother, was at the same school as her two sons. It seemed that Jonny knew them, but hadn't been aware straight away that their mother was my stepfather's sister. It must have been while they were talking about their families that Jonny worked out that the woman Jeanette's sons called their aunt was actually his own mother. Talk about a complicated situation because once Jonny was sure of that fact, he went round to Jeanette's house and asked if she would arrange for him to meet her. It was his dad, he insisted, who had stopped him trying to see his mother, which wasn't fair. Put like that, Jeanette told Mum, who could hardly refuse. Jeanette didn't know if she should mention it to her brother first, but instead decided to invite Mum over without explaining why – I suppose she didn't want to be caught up in any family problems. Though maybe she should have said why, though, because not letting either Mum or my stepdad know what she was arranging was a bit foolish, even for her – it could have caused a pretty big family row if it hadn't worked out.

Goodness knows what excuse she used to ask not just Mum but me as well to come over to her house when school was finished. According to Mum, it was not just afternoon tea we had been invited to, there was something else Jeanette wanted to discuss with her – 'But you can bring your homework with you and you can do it while Jeanette and I have a chat,' was all she said when she picked me up from school. I had been pretty surprised that she was there at the gate as it was not something she often did. Even when rainclouds turned the sky a dark grey and it was likely to rain heavily all day, she just told me to make sure I had my mac and brolly with me.

Looking back, I would say that Jeanette knew if she had been honest about the reason she was asking us over, even if Mum had gone, she would never have taken me with her. But evidently, Jonny had just about begged her to make sure I was there as well. Apart from Mum telling me that we were going to Jeanette's for tea, little else was talked about on that drive to my aunt's house.

Jeanette must have had an ear to the door for it swung open the moment we pulled up. 'Come on in, you two,' she said, giving us what even I thought was a bit of a nervous smile and without saying anything more, she led us straight into her kitchen. As part of her reason for us going over was that she wanted to talk to Mum, we were not expecting to see anyone else there, but sitting at the table was a dark-haired boy with a round freckly face who looked straight up at us. I might not have had a clue who he was, but from the way Mum gasped, I could tell she did. I heard her say to Jeanette 'Is that ...?' and before she could even finish the question, Jeanette just said, 'Yes, June.' And looking at me, she said with a tinge of triumph in her tone, 'Now, Ava, say hello to your brother Jonny.'

I was so amazed that I just froze for a moment, I couldn't think of a word to say as I stared at him. He didn't smile either, his eyes moved from Mum and just looked at me. I should think my eyes were wide with shock, for Mum's certainly were. It was not often I saw her looking vulnerable, but that day she did. Tears were forming in her eyes as she almost stuttered out the words, 'Jonny, is that really you?'

I didn't know what to say or do and just about whispered a 'hello'. Mum was looking just about ready to collapse as she pulled out the chair next to him. I don't remember much after those first few minutes, apart from Jonny saying I looked just like my dad. Mum, on the other hand, despite the shock, was clearly more than pleased to see him, which did make me think that my stepfather's story must have had some truth in it.

Seeing her talking to him quietly and his eyes glued to her face, I decided it would be better for them if they were left alone. Using my homework as an excuse, I went outside and began doing it on the metal table. It was Jeanette, when she brought me out a glass of lemonade and some cake, who tried to explain why she had arranged the meeting so secretly. As it wasn't up to me to criticise her, I just nodded and said nothing. It was only when she kept saying that Jonny had really wanted to meet me that I asked why because he had hardly said a word to me – 'I think he was just overwhelmed at seeing your mum again and meeting you,' was her answer, but it didn't quite convince me.

Once Mum came out to say it was time to go, I felt really disappointed that my brother hadn't come outside to talk to me – we just said goodbye to each other on the doorstep and that was it.

As Mum drove us home, there was a strange feeling of unease between us on the way back. In fact, the only time she spoke was to tell me it would be better if she told Ed about the visit and not me. I got the message and just muttered that I wouldn't say anything and I never did, but it bugged me that Jonny clearly hadn't been in the least bit interested in getting to know me, which made me just pin him down as being part of Mum's past and not mine.

So, was I hurt?

Yes, I was.

Back home, it didn't take more than a few days for the events of that afternoon to gradually slide to the back of my mind, almost as though nothing had happened. I never thought that we would meet up again, but I was wrong there for we did, when I was fifteen. And then it didn't take me long to realise what his real reason for wanting to see me had been.

30

The second event was when my older brother came into my life. But between me meeting both my brothers, my parents and I had one of the biggest rows ever, one that disturbed me far more than any of the other disagreements I had experienced before. And it was all to do with music, can you believe? Or rather my taste in it, which caused the beginning of a total wedge between my stepfather and me. One that I gave up even trying to resolve as I thought then – and still think now – that he had already made his decision not to attempt to either.

And how did it kick off? It was the music he found in my room. Music which I must have been listening to on my cassette player, the one I had been given for my tenth birthday. Of course it might have saved my bacon had it been an iPod complete with ear-phones so that only I could have heard the beat of the music I had become addicted to.

I must be fair here – it was Mum who had said that as I was entering my teens, I needed to have my own space. A place where I could do my homework, which would increase as I got older, and a place where I could read and listen to music, not to mention somewhere I could keep out of her way.

When friends of my parents and Mum's sister Aunty Mary knew about the present I was to be given, gift tokens were slipped into my birthday cards over the next few years. To begin with, Mum came along to the shops with me so that she could suggest what she saw as suitable music for someone my age, which meant she wanted to make sure I didn't choose anything my stepdad would find offensive – he simply hated anything modern, and rap and soul.

What my mother hadn't taken into account was that when I was a little older, my friends also helped me choose music that was more popular with our age group than her's. They simply copied it from their cassettes or CDs onto blank ones for me, which is why I ended up with a pretty mixed collection. By the time I turned thirteen, I was very much into urban R&B, soul music and also some hip hop and rap, which I admit did have a fair bit of swearing. But that was the type of music which was popular during my teens. What my parents didn't accept was that our generation had said goodbye to the nineties and welcomed in a far more liberal twenty-first century. I made sure when I was playing music that I turned it right down when my stepdad was around but when there was no one in, I would just pump up the volume of my favourites and dance around the room.

My stepdad did occasionally try to get me interested in some of the music he just about tolerated, such as the ballads from Boyzone: 'That's the sort you should be listening to. They've got good voices and they look neat and tidy as well, can't say that about many of the groups out there.' As I had more sense than to make any negative comments about his taste, he must have thought, or at least hoped, that I agreed with him. Except I don't think he did, otherwise why did he come into my room when I was downstairs to take a look at my music collection?

It was mainly the ones my friends had made for me that he pulled out first so he could run his eyes down the titles, which they had written on the sleeves. Unfortunately for me, one of the first ones he saw was a remake of a late sixties number, which back then had been top of the charts. 'Melting Pot' was originally sung by Blue Mink although a lot of well-known singers who approved of its ethos have recorded it since. He must have known from the title what the words in it were, because he didn't need to play it to just about go berserk at me for having it. It made him march to the top of the stairs and yell for Mum to come up to my room and bring me with him. As he was not a man who shouted often, I knew that I was in for it, but not why. Of course, Mum kept asking what I had done this time and my answer was, 'I don't know,' because I really didn't. What I did know was that she would give me no support at all.

When we reached my room, he was standing next to my cassette player, fuming. He didn't pick up the Blue Mink one first, instead he waved another one that Mum had given me in her face – 'See this cassette, June? She conned you into giving it to her, didn't she?'

'I told her to make a list of cassettes she wanted for her birthday and it was on in the shop I went into, that's all.'

'And you didn't ask your daughter or the shop assistant any questions about it?'

'No, I'm not that up to date with today's music, you know that.'

'Just listen to this load of disgusting rubbish then, June,' he snapped as he pressed 'play'. The profanities that came out on the first track did rather make me cringe – it was one thing being on my own and listening to it, another hearing them with those two in my room. Mum looked shocked when she realised that was what she had given me. All she had thought was it was music sung by a man named Eminem – and it wasn't at all the sort of music she had thought it was.

'Meaning you didn't get a good look at it. Told you she's not to be trusted and if you don't believe me, you will when you've heard the next one.'

With a sinking heart, I knew which cassette he had out – and it was that one that had made him so angry. 'Now if you thought that last song was bad, wait till you hear this one. I can hardly bear to listen to it myself,' he told her. Not that he walked out when it began playing, which I was wishing he would. 'Must have been one of her black friends that gave it to her.'

I didn't bother correcting him and telling him it was Hazel, the friend that Mum had approved of – that would have got her banned from the house too.

When he pressed the 'start' button, I listened to the words more than I had before. The 'Melting Pot' was a song about every colour of people in the world mixing together so that in the next century there would be 'coffee coloured people by the score'. To be truthful, I hadn't given the words much thought, I just liked the music and the name of the group, Blue Mink. But when I listened more intently, I felt it was a song trying to rid the world of racism, whereas my stepdad, on the other hand, saw it as trying to rid the world of white people. He pointed out aggressively to Mum, 'See, June, what it says – they want rid of our white race. To think it got banned in some countries and some radio stations here, now it's in your daughter's bedroom. Back then, decent folk protested and I was one of them, trying to stop it being played.'

Ed then went on to describe the comradeship within the groups of those who marched. He said the words were true racial hatred against all the whites and disrespectful to the proper British population: 'We are a white nation, always have been and always will be. Those immigrants think they have the right to come here and say they're British as well. Well, they haven't.'

I guess my stepfather's knowledge of political history was a little sparse, or perhaps he and his friends simply rewrote it. It was then that he shouted out that we should never have let the National Front go, they had the right ideas. A sentence that rang a bell in my head. For one of my school mates once asked me if my stepdad had even been a member of the National Front and I had said I didn't know.

Seeing his face turn purple with rage, I think my mother was concerned that he was going to have a heart attack. But I was scared, as he walked menacingly in my direction, that he was going to toss me out of the window. His anger was building up and he shouted louder and louder as he went on about me having a banned record when he had fought against it being played. It reminded me of what Hazel had said – it had only been banned from a couple of radio stations. Words like 'liberal scum who're trying to destroy us,' came pouring out before he carried on about those marches and how we needed more of them these days.

The last words he said to me sounded like a threat, that I should take care not to go against his principles. Mum finally managed to calm him down with promises of a drink to soothe their nerves. After telling me firmly to stay put, she led him out of my room but not before he repeated that the country should never have got rid of the National Front – 'They would have got more sorted!' he roared as he headed down the stairs.

Nothing could be the same after that; I had felt the heat of his hatred. Hatred of those who were not white and hatred for those who mixed with them.

And in his eyes, I was one of them.

31

After meeting Jonny, who I hadn't thought that I resembled one bit, I began to wonder what my older brother was like. Did he also look like our father? As Mum had either got rid of or hidden all the photos from her previous life, I hadn't seen any pictures of him. All I knew was that he was tall and we had the same colouring. I suppose it was that last row at home which had made me more curious. Deep down, I think that I must have been hoping that if we met, my other family might like me more than the one I was with.

My home life had really gone downhill after that scene. Mum was angry that she had taken some of the blame for me having the music my stepdad loathed and she flared up at the smallest excuse. She did her best to stop me having any social life at all by giving me so many chores to do, I hardly had any time for myself. Once, when I argued about not being allowed out after I had finished them, she slapped me hard across the face.

'You're staying in and that's that.'

When I watched her remove from my room some of the cassettes that had been given to me by my friends, I tried to stop her. Were they to be thrown out? I ran after her, saying, 'Please, Mum don't! There's nothing bad in those songs and some of them aren't even mine, they're on loan to me.'

'All black singers, aren't they?' she just about hissed before slapping me hard across the face for the second time since that confrontation.

It was then that I reached a stage of being really depressed – I just couldn't see a way out of it.

I knew Mum saw Jonny occasionally because her sister let that slip: 'Little bugger,' she had said, 'just goes round to Jeanette's house when he knows she's coming so that he can get extra pocket money from her.'

So, if Mum kept that quiet, maybe she was keeping other things to herself as well, though I knew better than to ask if she had heard anything from my older brother. I was in her bad books and couldn't see any possibility of getting out of them. When my end-of-term reports came in, she barely glanced at them before letting them slide out of her hands onto the table. Not a word uttered about my good grades and all my teachers praising me for my hard work and how I had applied myself to my studies. That day at Jeanette's house was never mentioned – she wanted me to forget all about it or so it seemed. And as I didn't want to make things even worse between us, I decided it was safer to pretend that I had. Only that wasn't true – how could it be?

Now these days I don't believe in the theory that if we wish for something hard enough, it will happen, but at thirteen, I sort of did. Because it was only about five or six weeks after I had met Jonny that my older brother Luke turned up. This time my stepfather would have been aware that he was coming – I wouldn't think Mum would have wanted to keep any secrets from him, especially now. It took him a while to forgive her for buying that cassette. Which was all fine, except no one had bothered to tell me.

Luke had already arrived before I got up. Which must have been the reason that, when I was leaving for school, I had the feeling someone was watching me. It was a strong enough feeling to make me spin round and look back at the house. *What the hell?* I wondered – for a second, I had thought I'd seen a man standing in one of our upstairs windows. Or was I imagining it? *What's a man doing in one of our bedrooms?* I asked myself as I hurried down the road, but by the time I reached school I didn't think much more about it. Once the bell rang, telling us school was over and we all rushed out, I was too busy chatting to friends who were walking in the same direction to give much thought to anything that had happened that morning. All I could think about was that I had left my house keys behind in my bedroom, which meant that I would have to go round the back to get in. I just hoped the gate was open – Mum would be really annoyed if she had to come to the door to let me in.

Just as I was feeling relieved to find the gate was unlocked, I saw a strange man sitting in our conservatory. Did I guess who he was? I think I must have. Because for some strange reason I only paused for a few seconds before I turned around and sprinted off to a friend's house. There, the pair of us managed to get most of our homework done before I reluctantly made my way home, two hours later.

Anyhow there was no sight of the man when I arrived back, which in a way disappointed me a little. And Mum, as usual, hardly said a word to me. I told her I had already done most of my homework, not that she seemed in the least bit interested. Grabbing the sandwich which had been left out for me, I went up to my room to change into my jeans – I never liked wearing my school clothes once I was home. It was only a little later when I heard Mum calling me to say that supper was nearly ready so I had better come down. Straight away, I noticed that she sounded far more friendly than she had for a while, so I guessed whoever the man was, she wanted me to meet him.

I gave my hair a quick brush before scuttling down the stairs and into the sitting room. And there was Mum, who told me that the man sitting on the sofa was my older brother, Luke. The moment my eyes met his twinkling ones, I found my face stretching into the widest smile possible. Without mentioning how I had sprinted off the first time he had seen me, his first words were, 'So, can I give my little sister a hug?' I walked up close to him and felt so happy when his arms went round me – he didn't just look nice, he smelt it as well. I knew at once that he and I were going to get on well and I was absolutely right there. When, after his hug, he held me at arm's length so we could have a good look at each other, I could see our facial similarities: he was tall and fit-looking, with twinkling green eyes and the same colour hair as me.

'Mum's invited me to stay the night,' he told me. 'So, how

about I walk with you to school tomorrow morning so we can chat on the way and get to know each other a bit?'

'That would be great,' I said, thinking there's nothing like showing off a handsome big brother to get some kudos with the other girls.

It was on our walk that he told me he had a vague memory of me when I was a baby. 'I was seven when Mum left,' he said with a smile, 'and you were a right little squawker. I suppose I was too young to realise that when she kissed both of us goodbye, she wasn't ever coming back.'

That was all he said then about her leaving, but over the times we met up, he admitted that he had really missed her. I could tell there was still a sadness in him about not seeing her as he was growing from a little boy to a young man and this is the reason I eventually plucked up my courage and asked why they hadn't met up much sooner.

'Oh, there were a few problems,' he answered and I accepted the fact that it was probably all he was going to say about it.

Over the next twelve months I was excited every time I heard he was visiting again and it was interesting to note that Ed seemed to make an effort to be friendly and he was careful as well – there was little alcohol consumed on those occasions and he kept his views on race and suchlike well hidden.

Once, Luke was waiting for me at the school gate and I just about whooped with joy. He never forgot my birthday either – it was never a day my parents made much fuss about because it seemed as if all that was reserved for my little sister, Dawn. And now that my adult life is more together and we have reconnected with each other, he is the wonderful brother who still supports me.

*   *   *

Let me be honest here: it's never easy to erase the past, that takes time, but we have to tell ourselves more than once that it's time to move on and we must fight to stop our past ruining our future. Maybe it was because I was determined to give my children a happy and secure background that gave me even more reason to put it all behind me. They needed a strong mother who could guide them through their early years so that one day, they would be confident, independent people. They also needed to feel that they had some family apart from me. It was then that I rang Luke.

Having changed my phone when I was with my ex, I had purposely lost contact with him. I was scared that he might turn up unexpectedly and see my bruises. He asked very few questions about why we had lost touch apart from where I was. Two days later, he came down for a visit. I told him everything. His response, apart from saying that he had no time for Jonny or my father, was to tell me not only was he married, but he had two children of his own.

'So, Ava,' he said, placing an arm around my shoulders, 'your two have two cousins as well as an aunt and uncle.' A family we see as often as we can.

32

It was Luke I went to and asked what the National Front was.

'What makes you ask me that? School giving you some social history questions, are they?' he said.

'No,' I answered carefully, 'someone at school asked me if Ed had been a member of them. You know, with him being a skinhead and stuff.'

I could tell he was petty shocked by that question.

'Not all skinheads were a part of that mob, Ava. Your stepdad might have agreed with some of their principles, but I doubt if he was ever a member, they were pretty hardcore.'

'So what were their principles?'

'Well, they believed that Britain is a country for white people and that our country would be a better place if the immigrants were sent back to where they had come from. The trouble was that those fiery ones in the National Front didn't work out that the countries the immigrants left were part of the Commonwealth so seeing Britain as their Mother country, they believed they would be welcome here.'

He then told me that there had been violent marches when

the Kenyan-Asians arrived in the UK in the late seventies: 'Seeing that they were well-educated people who, when Kenya gained its independence, chose to take British citizenship, they too thought they belonged here. As I said, the National Front were not very good at having a look at the real facts.' And he went on to talk about what subjects I liked best at school and I felt the subject had been subtly changed.

I could see he didn't want to tell me anything more about an organisation whose policies my stepfather, even if he had not been member, agreed with, but I knew where I could find all the information I wanted: in the library. So instead I asked him if it was true that the National Front had got the song 'Melting Pot' banned.

Luke just laughed at that. 'Oh, that song! Yes, there was a bit of a fuss and a few complaints to a couple of radio stations, which made some of them stop playing it. But no, there were no marches as far as I know. Don't think it was the type of music that lot would have been listening to anyhow.'

Maybe I should have let it rest, but I was curious about what the National Front stood for and what they had done. I told Mum I was going to the library because I needed to do some research for history, which might have been true, even though it was not the era she would have thought I would have been looking at. And by the end of an hour in the library I had found what I read distressing. Marching against the lyrics of a song was one thing, but firebombing black and Asian people's homes? Attacking people and putting them in hospital? As I walked home, I felt stunned.

Now you might ask why I have put that information in

my story. The answer is that it explains my stepdad's beliefs, which had, especially since I was a teenager, affected my life – and in the long run, would have a huge effect on the lives of my children.

33

It was when my fourteenth birthday was coming up that I was actually asked what I would like for it. Tempted as I was, I knew better than to say some more music to replace the cassettes you threw in the bin. Instead I tried to look as meek as possible and told my parents I'd really love a Nokia phone – you know, one of those ones that twenty years ago could only be used for making calls or sending messages. Back then, they were modern and every teenager wanted one. I didn't think I had a chance of getting one, but I kept my fingers crossed in the hope that I would.

When I came down for breakfast, to my surprise my parents and my sister were waiting for me with smiles and happy birthday wishes. Not only that, there were several envelopes with birthday cards in them as well as two prettily wrapped parcels. I opened the one my little sister said was from her, first. And I gave a gasp of pleasure when I saw the delicate silver charm bracelet inside it. Mum might have paid for it, but Dawn made sure to tell me she had chosen it. Not only that, she had made me a birthday card with hearts on it: 'My teacher helped me with it.' I was so pleased with both the present and the card that I felt a lump forming in my throat. Jumping up from my seat, I gave her a hug.

When I removed the wrapping from the other parcel, there was the phone I had wanted for so long, fitted inside an oblong box.

'Means I can always ring you and ask where you are,' Mum said, only this time it was more of a joke than anything else, which made me grin back at her.

'And here's another one,' my stepfather said, passing me an envelope. Inside was a card with a book token inside; it was from Luke. That made me think of one of the phone's good points: now I would be able to ring him to thank him.

That morning was about the first time we had all chatted away at the breakfast table without any undercurrents of my parents' disapproval of my lifestyle. Mind you, I had already managed to scrape into their good books a little. OK, you might think what I did was rather devious, but I couldn't stand the situation of hardly being spoken to much longer. So, what did I do? I asked a couple of my white friends to do me a favour and call round to see me.

They were pretty horrified when I told them why.

'You mean some of our other friends are not allowed to come round to your house, Ava?'

'That's right.'

'Might have known an old skinhead who still rides a motorbike would be like that,' said Hazel, who my mother had met a few times and approved of. We all laughed together.

'Have to mind my P's and Q's as well,' said Jenny, my other friend.

'And please don't mention music whatever you do.' I told them. 'They have a thing about black singers.'

'I bet!' was Hazel's comment, swiftly followed by, 'what else do we expect from skinhead racists?'

It was a good thing that they understood that although my parents' views were not something I agreed with, I didn't have much choice but to tolerate them for now. Having both of them calling around to see me just might have been the reason the phone jumped into my lap. Mum certainly approved of them and kept telling me what nice girls they were.

* * *

So, who was the first person I called on my phone? My brother Luke, of course.

'Can't believe you have a phone now,' he told me laughingly, as we chatted away. Since I had met him, I wished he lived nearer but at least having a phone meant I could make a call without our conversation being overheard.

It was him who I finally asked for our father's phone number. Since my birthday, I had been brooding about him. I had even hoped that there would be at least a card from him too. Now I had met my brothers, I wanted to get to know my father too – the last piece of the puzzle that remained unknown and I was desperate to meet him.

'Are you sure, Ava?' Luke asked when I explained why

I wanted the number. 'Could get you in big trouble – and me as well.'

'I know that but there's no way they can find out, Luke. I'm pretty careful. And if I was caught, I'd say it was in the directory.'

Before he could reply, I couldn't stop myself from asking my next question: 'Do you think he will be pleased to hear from me?' I could tell from his hesitation in giving me the number that he had a reason for not wanting to.

'You know, sometimes it's better to let things lie, Ava. I know your parents and understand you have had your difficulties with them, but contacting our dad would be like putting petrol on a smouldering fire.'

'But, Luke, he's my dad, isn't he? Like Mum is your mum and you wanted to meet her, so why shouldn't I?'

That must have placed Luke between a rock and a hard place. He most probably could think of a dozen reasons why I shouldn't contact my real father, but then hadn't he reached out to Mum against his wishes? Luke wasn't the type of man who would have run our father down, though later I'm sure he wished he had told me more of the truth.

He reluctantly gave me the number and again told me to be careful: 'You don't need any more upsets in your life, now do you?' Not that he explained what they could be, though I doubt if at fourteen I would have listened to him anyhow. Once I had that number scribbled down, nothing and no one was going to stop me making that call.

'Let me know how it goes anyhow, Ava, and you know I'm here for you, don't you?' he said finally.

'Yes,' was all I could think of to say for I was too excited to take on board that those words were his way of warning me.

And that's when my secret calls to my dad began.

I can picture myself now, standing in the park, where no one could overhear me, dialling a number without knowing who would answer it. Would it be my brother Jonny, Dad's new wife Liza or my father who would pick up the call? If it was his wife, what would I say? That I wanted to speak to her husband? Would she even know who I was? And if it was Jonny, I would have no option other than to hang up. Couldn't risk him telling Mum, could I?

But I needn't have been so bothered about who would be on the other end of the line, because it was my father who answered. I was so completely lost for words it's a wonder he didn't drop it back on the cradle, thinking it must be a prank call. Screwing up all my courage I managed to blurt out, 'It's me, Ava. You know, your daughter.'

For a few seconds all I could hear was his breathing and then he took a deep breath and said, 'Ava, my goodness, what a surprise!' By the tone of his voice I was pretty certain he meant that it was a nice one. Of course, I had a whole heap of questions I wanted to ask him, the main one being why he never tried to see me. But I didn't. Instead he gently asked me a couple of questions of his own, which got me talking. He sounded really impressed when I told him about my swimming training and how I had won several prizes.

To my absolute joy he asked me if I would like to meet him. Would I? Of course I would, more than anything. When I told him that I would love to do so, he sounded really pleased.

He asked about when my lunch break was, then we arranged for us to meet up later in the week. When we said goodbye, he sounded so warm and friendly, I just about jumped with joy.

All I could think about the night before we had arranged to meet was that I was finally going to meet my real dad. Never had I tried so hard to look so smart for school before. I told one of my teachers that my dad was coming to see me, not that I explained which one it was. That got me excused from my last lesson of the morning and I was given written permission to leave the school premises. When the midmorning bell rang, telling me I had a whole hour and a half free, I flew out of the classroom – I had never rushed so fast to get through those school gates.

Even if he hadn't been the only man standing outside the gates, I would have recognised him straight away. Mum was right, I had taken after him in looks. He was almost an older version of Luke, I thought, except for his faded pale bronze hair and eyes that were not quite so twinkling. Weird really, seeing a man you had never met before who looks just like you.

Smile and hugs came in my direction before he told me that I had better have something to eat. He took me to a hotel bar, where he ordered something called a club sandwich for me and a soft drink. He even offered me a cigarette and wanting to look grown-up, I took it. I almost choked, but somehow managed to try and look an old hand when he leant forward and lit it for me. Our first conversation convinced me not only did we look alike but we had similar tastes in music and the same beliefs about other cultures as well. And like most fourteen-year-olds, I was naive enough to think that was totally amazing. He made me feel that I could tell him anything, which I really believed I could. He even invited me to visit him at his home but I couldn't accept – I just didn't dare.

*　*　*

For the next ten months, my father drove over to see me often and I felt there was a real closeness building up between us. My world was turning into a happier place with the belief that I had a father who wanted to spend time with me. He had told me I could tell him everything and I must have done just that. I poured out about how I didn't get on with my stepfather and about him not liking my taste in music. Oh, he was really sympathetic then: 'I dislike that man more than I can say,' he told me. 'He had an affair with my wife, your mum, when she was pregnant with you.' I sort of knew that, but not his version, which he went on to tell me. 'That was such a horrible day,' he said, looking sad, 'when I came home from work to find both her and you gone.' He then told me about what he thought about how she had left her two young sons behind.

He made himself out to be the victim and I totally believed him.

*　*　*

It was the same year I received my phone that everything at home became much worse. In my youthful head it had reached a stage where being there was more than I could bear. There was constant disapproval of my life. It seemed as if inviting a couple of my white girlfriends to visit me hadn't been enough to get them off my case. I began to feel that my stepfather was asking his friends to keep their eyes open and when they saw me, they reported back to him. Because I definitely hadn't seen Ed at the time he said he had seen me walking in what he called, 'a mixed group'.

'Can't you white kids just walk with other white ones?' was the question he kept firing at me.

'They are just my classmates,' was the answer I gave every time.

'That's no excuse. Seems those nice white English girls you brought here have no sense either. I suppose they have loony lefties for parents. Bloody liberals! I can only hope for their sakes that they all have decent morals – they need to know what people think and stop mixing with them.'

I wanted to say it's how you and your racist biker friends think, not other normal people. We lived in Leicester for God's sake, a very diverse town. Of course I knew only too well that there was some racism in the school. It's not as though the town was a perfect one but our school did their best to stamp it out. Not all our teachers were white either, which helped put a stop to it. Not my stepdad though, that just made something else for him to become angry about.

What I was completely unaware of then was that he had been scared of what might happen once I was at senior school. Hence the talk he had given me just before I began there. He had seen and been told by those who shared his opinions how groups of young teenagers mixed together.

To him, the absolute worst thing that might happen was me ending up with a boyfriend who wasn't white.

It was just as well that Ed hadn't guessed that I was already more than a little infatuated with a mixed-race guy named Greg, who was part of our group. With his slicked-back, dark wavy hair, smooth skin and sparkling dark brown eyes, I thought he was absolutely gorgeous. So, what did I do to try and get his attention? The same as most teenage girls do the first time they fancy someone of the opposite sex: put on some lip gloss and flirt at every opportunity. It seemed to take forever to get him to notice me, even though I could hardly take my eyes off him. Each time a smile from him came in my direction or he actually spoke to me, I went weak at the knees. And of course I didn't stop hoping that him being friendly would lead to something else – which eventually it did.

It was during the summer holidays that we began hanging out together. Leaving the house in the daytime was not too much of a problem as Mum and my stepdad would both be out working. My sister, who was still too young to be left alone in the house, was ferried over to our Aunt Mary's home on their way to work. A couple of times a week I joined her there so I could spend time with my cousins. I think Mum believed I was either at Aunt Mary's or with Jenny and Hazel, but she was wrong there! Dad drove over around once a week to see me, while I met up with Greg on most of the other days.

My visits to his house began with Greg inviting me over to watch a movie. Good thing he had a really good video shop nearby and he let me choose. It might have taken me the best part of an hour to get to him, but to me it was well worth the walk. Especially as after a couple of visits a bit of cuddling came into the equation, followed by some kissing. Right from that first kiss I was convinced I had discovered just what true love was. He was the very first person who had brought out those feelings in me, so I was in love, wasn't I? That's what I kept telling myself anyhow. Which might have been all right if I had kept that thought to myself. But no, I had to go and tell my real father all about Greg and my feelings for him.

He sounded really enthusiastic about every detail I gave him; said he thought it was really great I had a boyfriend. 'And,' he added, 'from what you've told me he's sounds really nice and keen on getting good grades too so you should be proud of him for that. Certainly, makes me feel good to see my daughter looking so happy. Might be walking you up the aisle one day.' He then gave me a wink that made me giggle.

Well, at least one parent thought my choice of boyfriend was a good one. One who knew his opinion would be the complete opposite of the man Mum had left him for. My confidence was really boosted after that conversation: he was my real dad so shouldn't it be him who I listened to? I should have taken on board the fact that real dad or not, he had totally ignored me for fourteen years. Whether I shared my parents' beliefs or not, my stepfather was the one putting food on the table and nice clothes on my back. Which is not the way many teenagers think, any more than they are good at hiding their emotions. One moment they look as if they are in a dream and the next off they go, phone in hand, to make a private call before returning with big soppy grins on their faces.

My head was too full of Greg to stop myself letting my guard down. It hadn't taken Mum long to work out there was someone in my life who mattered – the combination of lip gloss and dreamy expression must have given the game away. It was her job to try and get me to tell her who it was I had been spending time with. I'm sure she hoped it was one of the white boys at the swimming club that she had tried so hard to get me to show an interest in.

Maybe if I hadn't just come first in a race there amid a few cheers, I might have managed to say 'No one, Mum,' when she asked me who it was. But according to her, I blushed bright red when she asked his name. Without thinking, the name 'Greg' came out of my mouth, though I did say we were just good friends and his family were really nice too.

Now the name Greg might have sounded British, but Mum was not so easily fooled: 'He's not part of your swimming team then?'

'No,' I said.

'So is he in the same class as you at school?'

'Yes.'

'And are we talking about a white or a black boy, Ava?'

'His mother's white,' I managed to say, not thinking that would make matters even worse.

'Is she now, and what colour is the boy's father?'

'Not black, Mum, he's Asian.'

'I thought he would be. Your dad saw you with that boy when a group of you were walking home from school and I have to tell you he was not very impressed.'

My heart was literally sinking. I knew then that I had made a big mistake but I couldn't lie at this point and so I admitted he was the one I was chatting to after school.

'Mmm! And you were smart enough not to have him anywhere near the house, weren't you? Which tells me you knew what the consequences would be if Ed had seen you with him.'

'It's not like that, Mum, we're only friends,' I protested.

'He's the one you spent a lot of time with over the summer holidays, I expect. Don't take me for a fool, Ava.' She looked more worried than angry as she continued, 'What you've got to understand is that Ed will never accept you having a coloured boyfriend. It will cause huge problems in the house if he gets to know about it. So be sensible: if you break it off with him now, I won't tell him. But, Ava, if you don't, it won't take him long to find out and you know just how angry he can get if you disobey us.'

I felt that I had no choice but to cave in and say I wouldn't see him on my own. After that scene about my taste in music, I certainly didn't want to go through another one like it, only I couldn't bring myself to keep my word.

For a while I still managed to see Greg after school. He accepted the fact that once the holidays were over, I had an eight o'clock curfew. What I didn't tell him was that my parents insisted on knowing where I was. Back then, locations could not be tracked on mobile phones, so I felt I was pretty safe. Which didn't stop me lying to Mum and getting my friends to cover for me. I should think everyone in our class knew about us, which made me hold my head up high.

Until I was caught, that was.

First, it was Mum who went ballistic at me breaking my promise. She told me she had seen us walking together when she was driving home from work. 'We weren't doing anything wrong,' I insisted, 'we're in the same class so have the same homework. We were only in the library looking up some stuff to help with our assignment.'

Which actually was completely true.

'Hardly seems something a boy would want to do once you've broken it off with him.'

'But he's only a friend, Mum.'

'I don't care what you call him, Ava. I'm telling you for the last time, break it off. If I catch you with him one more time, I will have to tell Ed.'

My mother's attempts to control me were taken out of her hands when my stepfather spotted Greg and me walking together in the opposite direction to our house. When he told Mum, all she could say was that I had been told not to see him alone. My stepfather was no fool either – he had seen the way we were smiling at each other and how our hands were just about touching. That was enough, he told me, to tell him that we were not just friends.

And that's when all hell broke loose. My mother, realising that my stepdad was just about to lose his temper, shot out of the room. Which told me that she saw no reason to protect me. My relationship with my stepdad might not have been anything like as good as when I was a little girl, but still, I had never seen such fury on his face before and for the first time I felt really frightened by him.

'Don't bother lying to me, Ava. That boy I saw you with outside the school is the one you've been seeing, isn't he?'

'He's a friend,' was my answer.

'I said don't lie to me, Ava! He's more than that, isn't he? Now for once listen to me, because this is your last chance to have a good life. Let me tell you what decent people will think when they see you with that boy. That you're another little scrubber throwing her life away. Do you know what they'll call you? There won't be any decent man who will respect you. And, Ava, that means me as well. Now I'm telling you, don't go near him anymore, do you understand?'

'But, Dad, we've not been doing anything wrong, we've only kissed.'

'You think? Well, I'm not having it. It will bring shame on this family and destroy your sister's life as well as yours. The very idea of how they came to exist makes me feel sick. And as for them being allowed to marry in church and take their Christian vows there, all I can say is there should be a law against it – would be if me and my friends had anything to do with it.'

He made it very clear to me that there was no way I was going to creep out of the house and see that boy. That while I lived at home I was never to go into a house where a woman like that boy's mother lived. He accepted I might have to say the odd word to him at school, but I was never to meet him on my own: 'And if you think that walking with a mixed group like that would help, don't even contemplate of it. You just hurry home.' By now he was almost purple in the face as rage and hatred overwhelmed him.

I felt completely shattered after he had finished this tirade and rushed up to my room. But that was by no means the end of it: Mum came up to inform me of my new house rules. I was not allowed out of the house at weekends unless I was accompanied by her. I must come straight home from school, no chatting and walking with a group. And she would know if I had – they would be watching me as would others. And not only could I not visit anyone, no one could visit me.

The only bit of a break I had was when Mum took me to her sister's. Not out of kindness, I knew, but because she no longer trusted me. Apart from those visits, my weekends were taken up with homework and the multitude of chores I was given to do.

* * *

For weeks, I felt so sad. Not being able to spend time with any of my friends was driving me mad. It's a wonder my parents hadn't thought to take my phone off me – I think that was probably because they didn't want Luke to be unable to contact me. He told me that he had heard about me not being allowed out: 'Just go along with them for now and I'll be coming to see you soon.'

When the call ended, I felt even more miserable though I had to admit to myself there was nothing much he could do to help me.

I hated my parents for what they were putting me through.

And as for Mum, especially, all respect for her had disappeared. That was mainly because I had overheard Aunty Betty telling her that Greg was a nice boy and his father was a very well-respected man in the area – 'He's a doctor, for heaven's sake, June!'

'Doesn't matter who he is, Ed won't change his mind.'

'You never had those racist opinions before you met him, did you?' she challenged.

'That's the way life is. I'm not going to disagree with him and that's that. Anyway, a lot of what he says is probably right.'

Yes, I thought miserably, *you've put him before me, like you always have.*

* * *

Just when I thought my life couldn't get any worse, it did. Greg kept trying to get me to have a chat outside school or to come to his house, or just walk around a bit together. None of which I dared agree to. I used as many excuses as I could until he stopped making suggestions.

The last time he tried was when he told me his mum had invited me over for tea and I blurted out that I wouldn't be allowed to go.

'You mean your stepdad saw you with me, don't you? And you've gone along with his National Front racist views, haven't you?'

'No,' I tried to say, but I was too late – Greg had turned on his heels and walked away.

That was when I knew just how much I hated my stepdad.

And it was that feeling that made me make another mistake: I phoned Dad.

I was so angry and hurt, when he picked up the phone I couldn't stop myself from bursting into tears. I begged him to come and get me when school was over and he did. I had done it, I was free – I could be friends with whoever I wanted, no shame, no racism, just normality.

Or so I thought.

34

On the morning when I made that phone call, I hadn't given any thought to what I wanted to happen. Which is not surprising seeing as one moment I was in floods of tears, the next I was full of rage. It was the second when I walked up and down my room cursing my parents that caused enough adrenaline to shoot into my veins until I was so wired up, I couldn't keep still. And I certainly didn't have a clear thought in my head. Did I really want to leave home, say goodbye to my friends, my aunt, my cousins, my little sister and even my mum? If I hadn't asked myself that, at least I should have found out if Dad really wanted me as part of his family. Because if he didn't, what would happen to me then? Unfortunately for me, I did not hesitate in my belief that he did.

The other thought that should have registered in my mind was how he, a responsible adult, was prepared to drive me away from my school and home without discussing it with Mum first. I mean, I was underage. So how much worry would my absence give them? But no, I didn't give a thought to any of this. Instead I packed everything I could manage into my rucksack, gulped down my breakfast and then made my way to school – the school where there were classes I needed to attend so I could take my GCSEs in less than two years. Something else I didn't stop and think about, even though I had been told countless times that a good education gives us independence. I suppose I have to make some excuses for my younger self: she was only just turning fifteen and feeling that no one was on her side. Having been made to give up her first love, she was hurting at the unfairness of it all. That day all that was in my mind was how my parents had stopped me from living the life of a normal teenager.

Dad, true to his word, turned up at lunchtime. *Goodbye, school*, I thought as I ran towards his car. Once I jumped in, the smile on my face disappeared as I burst into tears.

'Think we'd better have a chat before we get to my home,' he said, pulling out some tissues from the glove compartment and passing them to me. 'We'll go and get a coffee and you'd better have something to eat as well. In the meantime, take one of my cigarettes – that will calm you a little,' he told me as he drove towards the hotel where we had gone the first time we met. By now I had got used to smoking when we were together, not that I smoked any other time.

Once we were inside the hotel lounge and our order had been taken, he told me I had better tell him exactly what had gone so wrong at home. He appeared really sympathetic when I began explaining. When I glanced up at him he was looking at me so intently that it made me feel he recognised what I was feeling and really felt for me. That sort of understanding was something that neither parent had ever shown much of.

It made me feel all tearful again and was enough to make me spill absolutely everything out.

Such as how my mother didn't love me because I looked like him. A statement that made him smile wryly. That was a remark she made nearly every time she got drunk, I told him as all loyalty to my parents disappeared. I even told Dad the things that had been said about him by both my parents. How Mum kept telling me that it was not just his looks I had, but his character as well and that was not a good one. Oh no, I didn't hold anything back. I could hardly stop another flood of tears coming when I told him not only was my relationship with my mother almost non-existent, but my stepfather, who once I had felt loved by, now saw me as bringing disgrace on the family.

'He makes me feel suffocated,' I told him. 'I know he gets those friends of his to spy on me. They tell him straight away if I'm seen chatting to someone who isn't white. Like a classmate, not even a boyfriend, and you can imagine how unpopular I would be if I refused to talk to them. He's been like that ever since I went to senior school. I can't even go to a friend's house to do homework. He doesn't even like my white friends now, says they're also mixing with the wrong people.

'I've not been allowed out for ages. Not on my own anyhow, only with Mum. I used to have loads of friends, but now a whole bunch who are friends with Greg are snubbing me. They're saying I'm getting as bad as my racist stepdad.'

I then told him about those horrible words Ed had used when he told me why, if I carried on as I had been, no man would ever respect me and that meant him as well.

'You're nothing like that, are you, Dad?' I asked him shakily.

'Of course not, sweetheart. Told you I can't stand the man and I loathe all bigots but especially racists. Your mum was never like that before she met him,' he told me before he changed the subject.

'Now, Liza is looking forward to meeting you and so is Jonny. You met him a while back. didn't you? Oh, I know it was meant to be a secret, but secrets have a knack of coming out.'

'That's true,' I said, thinking of mine with Greg.

'Well, you'll be pleased to hear that he's not forgotten you. He's told me how much he's looking forward to meeting you again though I don't know why you haven't met up before now, seeing he's managed to visit your mum quite a few times. Not that he's going to go over there anymore – that was something I had to put my foot down about. And no, I don't want to give you the reasons, just that it wasn't doing him any good.'

I told Dad that I was looking forward to seeing him again too, which was not strictly true as it was really Luke I wished to see. So, I mentioned to Dad how much I enjoyed Luke's company and asked whether he was likely to visit.

'What did he tell you about our family?'

'He didn't say much at all. Why, Dad?'

'Just wondered. I'm pleased for you, it must be nice to have a big brother.'

'It is, Dad – I can't tell you how wonderful it is.'

'No doubt he'll come over when you let him know where you are.'

The expression on Dad's face remained fairly cheerful for he had no intention of letting me know that he and his elder son were often at loggerheads. In fact, I was to find out later that once Luke had left home, he very rarely visited. I didn't notice how quickly Dad changed the subject as he then began talking about their house; how even though they had spent many months renovating it, there was still more work to be done: 'I have some photos at home which show you what it looked like when we bought it. Just an old barn really that we're slowly turning into a real home. And talking of home, the family's waiting for you to arrive though I know you've spoken to Liza already.'

Which was true. A couple of times when I had rung Dad, it had been she who answered. She seemed so happy and excited to hear from the long-lost daughter her husband had told her about. At the time I had so much anger towards my own mother that it felt comforting to hear that they were so pleased I had managed to be back in his life. Here was a woman I could talk to without getting her disapproval, I felt. It was that and Dad's warmth and friendliness towards me which reinforced my fantasy of becoming part of a loving family.

This is the beginning, I told myself. *He's taking me to live with them.* I was convinced that I was really wanted there. I suppose it sounds pathetic, doesn't it? But then I just wanted to feel loved, for I really craved it. I suppose not being quite fifteen, I was at an age where the slightest gesture of kindness could easily win me over.

35

I spent most of my time looking out of the window during that drive to Dad's house, watching how the scenery changed, as we drove through the outskirts of Leicester into more of a rural part of the county. To the right and left of us all I could see were fields with cows or sheep grazing or freshly dug soil, where crops had been planted.

On the way he pulled up into a layby and rang Liza to tell her that we were only about twenty minutes away before handing me the phone: 'She wants to speak to you,' he told me as I took hold of it.

Liza chatted away to me while I held the phone up to my ear, telling me how much she and Jonny were looking forward to my arrival. And that she had seen some photos of me and didn't I look a lot like my father? All of which made me feel excited at the prospect of meeting them.

'Nearly there,' Dad said as we drove through a pretty village before turning down what looked more like a lane than a road and he pulled his car up right at the end of it. 'Here we are,' he said smiling and my eyes popped wide open at the sight of the house. Part-wood, part-brick with large picture windows, it was much bigger than I had expected.

Liza must have heard us pull up for just as I opened the car door and climbed out of my seat, I saw a petite, pretty woman dressed in jeans and a T-shirt rushing towards us while behind her their five-year-old daughter Eve was doing her best to keep up. *A miniature version of her mother*, I thought, seeing the same dark hair and wide smile. The first thing I noticed about Liza was that she was undeniably pregnant; something my dad seemed to have forgotten to tell me about. The second was that, with her dark hair pulled back into a high ponytail and her lightly tanned, smooth face, she was a lot younger than him.

Talk about an effusive welcome; she was all smiles as she greeted me and said she could hardly believe how pretty I was. As we walked in, I couldn't get over the size of the kitchen. A huge cream oven of a type I had never seen before was set against one wall.

'It's called an Aga,' Liza told me when she saw me staring at it. 'It's the best thing to cook with. Only we cheated a bit, it runs on gas.' What I was more interested in was the wonderful cooking aroma in the air and then she opened one of the doors to the Aga to let me see inside one of its four ovens. A simmering chicken casserole smelt so delicious, it made my stomach rumble. She gave me a hug before taking me upstairs to show me my bedroom, where a double bed took up most of the room. It had been Luke's room before he left home, she explained.

'The wardrobe's a bit full because when Luke left, I hung

a lot of my clothes in it. Still, you haven't brought much with you,' she noted.

That was true, I didn't have room in my rucksack to bring more.

'But it has its own shower room,' she added, opening a door to a lovely little bathroom. 'Expect you would like to freshen up.'

Once Liza had gone back downstairs I had a long hot shower and changed. Getting out of my school clothes and into jeans and a light jumper made me feel better. I have to say that first night there was great. Even little Eve wanted my attention. I felt so welcome and Dad appeared to be proud of having a daughter who clearly thought the world of him. I was convinced that he was a really lovely father and wished Mum had stayed with him. Wouldn't we have all been happier if it was he who had brought me up? And as for Liza, she seemed so nice and genuinely friendly. They both appeared really supportive about what I had been through and eager to know as much as possible about me and my family.

Jonny, who came in a little later, appeared rather different from the young boy I had met just a few years earlier. He had grown taller, seemed more confident but his face was still freckly, only this time he smiled and told me how happy he was to see me again. And I really thought he meant it.

It was he who asked me if our mother knew where I was.

'No,' said Dad, looking rather embarrassed. 'Ava was so upset when I met up with her, I decided to give her a break from that vile stepfather of hers. I'll phone the police now and ask them to let them know.'

'Oh, no need for that, Dad – I can ring Mum's sister Mary and she'll tell them. Doubt if they've noticed I've even gone yet. Maybe they think I'm round at someone's house where I'm not supposed to be,' I said.

'The police are better, Ava – they will just do their job. And that means Ed can't report you missing. Never know what that man might decide to do.'

I didn't know then what the message was that he wanted to be given to my stepdad, but I do now. Dad told the police that I had contacted him. He thought I had told Mum I was going to visit him for a few days, or he wouldn't have taken me away without her permission but of course he would take me home after the weekend and he hoped that was OK with them.

A text came onto my phone about an hour later. It was my stepdad and he responded to Dad's message via the police: 'Ava, you have burnt your bridges now. You can stay where you are, you are not wanted here.'

It was the shock of that last message from my stepfather that brought tears to my eyes. Wasn't he the man who had said that he had loved me ever since I was a tiny baby? All right, there had been some terrible rows, not just with him, but with Mum as well. But how could they say that I was no longer welcome in their home? Wasn't it mine too?

Not anymore, my inner voice told me sadly.

I don't know how I managed not to show how upset I was, but I did. It was when I went to bed and looked at the message again that I cried my eyes out, shuddering with huge uncontrollable sobs. I wanted to delete it but I couldn't bring myself to do so. By now I was really feeling muddled and confused emotionally. Had I really thought that I could run off to Dad without making them more than angry? It was the shock of that message that frightened me. However furious my stepfather had been with me, I had still believed that underneath it all, he still loved me. And Mum, what about her? And then I remembered something her sister Betty had said: "She will always put him first, Ava." So, I had tested my mother and found out to my cost, that her sister knew her better than I did.

I know now that it was a warning, but then I didn't. My teenage head had never taken in that my stepfather might want rid of me and that he would use the fact of my going off with my father as an excuse not to have me back. All I could think was that the situation I was in was out of my hands.

It took several days before I felt able to show the text to Liza and then everything changed. My heart sank when I saw the expression on her face alter to something close to fury. It hardly took any time at all before she began to reveal her true self – a completely different person to the one who had been so warm and welcoming the day I arrived.

It didn't take me long to realise that it was one thing having a guest who she could charm for a few days, but not one it looked as though she could be stuck with indefinitely. To make things even clearer, she told me that the only reason Dad had been seeing me was to get back at Mum: 'When you made that last call all choked up with tears, he could hardly wait to bring you here. He's never forgiven her for leaving him. So now you know.'

And now I did.

'Ava, you invented a father who didn't exist,' she said a little more gently. 'I expect when things went wrong in your family you thought he was the one to rescue you. I suppose you're not old enough to ask yourself why he never tried to see you. Well, now I'm going to tell you the truth: it was because he forgot about you, but he never forgot about your bitch of a mother.'

So, she was jealous of Mum even after all those years and nothing was going to make her accept me.

Liza, being a woman who had no intention of not getting her own way, soon made it clear that I could not stay with them. Whatever she had said about my father, I still felt that there was something between us. I was upstairs in my room when I heard them arguing. Opening my door slightly, their voices became clearer.

'Don't say we're stuck with her!' Liza yelled.

At least she called me down for supper later, not that I can remember a word that was said or what we ate.

For the next few days when both Dad and Jonny were out, she just ignored me. When I walked into the kitchen, she walked out. What did I do to her? I didn't understand this behaviour – I had tried ever since I had been there to be polite and helpful.

'You're like your mother,' she told me more than once when I offered to clear dishes or pack the dishwasher.

What did that mean? Looking back, I guess she did not want my father paying me any attention when she already had a daughter and another child on the way. I just didn't understand how one night I went to sleep feeling secure there, only to wake up to an angry, resentful woman who didn't want me there for a single day longer. In the end she made my father choose to have either a peaceful home or one with continuous rows.

He chose peace.

It was Liza who, with a triumphant expression on her face, came into my bedroom before the household was up: 'You're leaving so get out of bed and pack. My husband's going to take you back before he goes to work.'

So, he was her husband now and not my father. No breakfast was mentioned. Oh, Dad said he was sorry that he had to take me back so soon – it had only been about ten days. Not as sorry as I was, but he was sure Mum would be pleased to see me. Then he told me he had sent her a text, telling her he was bringing me back.

'What did she say? Is she still angry with me?' I asked, fearing the answer.

'She didn't reply but then, I'm not someone she would want to have any communication with,' he said.

I had hoped he would say something more to comfort me, but he didn't. He had made his choice and I had no alternative but to do as I was told. Out of the corner of my eye I could see Liza standing there, a pleasant smile on her face. She said her goodbyes to me, though unlike my warm welcome, this time there were no hugs – just her parting words, 'Take care of yourself.'

Little was said on that journey home. Well, I suppose there was nothing to say really. As Liza had told me, I had built up the image of the perfect father in my head, one that did not exist. Now he seemed almost like a stranger. Even though I felt that he had taken me away to get his own back on Mum, there had been something special between us that was now gone. Surely it wasn't all a pretence, it couldn't have been? Deep down, I felt he was sorry to let me go. For he must have been aware that after Liza's aggression towards me; our long phone calls were over, as were our meetings.

If I had heard excuses like my parents had texted him and said they were sorry and were upset and wanted me back, I might have understood it. But there were no such excuses, just that neither he nor Liza wanted me in their home any longer.

'Best if your mum doesn't see me,' he said without meeting my eye as he dropped me off in the street behind what I still thought of as home. Without saying a word and after slinging my rucksack on my shoulders, I started walking towards the house. I must have been shaking a bit with nerves as I kept wondering what their reaction would be: would I have to stay in even more now or would they give me back some of my freedom?

I'll soon find out, I told myself as I walked up the path.

Something was wrong, for when I got to the house they weren't in. I rang the bell who knows how many times, but no one answered. Back down the drive I went and called at a neighbour's house. There was a dull feeling of apprehension creeping up from my stomach; they knew I was coming, so why weren't they in? I checked my phone and there were no messages for me except the one text my stepdad had sent when I first arrived at Dad's home, telling me that I had burnt my bridges.

The neighbour told me she had no idea where they were. She hadn't seen them that morning. And no, they hadn't left a key for me.

Now what? I asked myself, beginning to feel really sick, so I rang Hazel, who was the friend who lived the nearest to me, who simply said, 'Come over.'

Hazel as usual was really kind. Seeing I looked a little shaky, she put her arm around my shoulder and told me to follow her up to her room – 'I can see you have loads to tell me, seeing you've skipped school.'

As soon as we were out of her mother's earshot, she asked me where I had been for nearly two weeks. That was enough to make me blurt absolutely everything out amid a few hiccupping gulps and enough tears to need a whole bunch of tissues. She told me to wait in her room as she was going to ask her mum to ring my parents and see what was going on.

'But they're out.'

'Maybe they're back now.'

Of course they were in, as Hazel's mother found when she made the phone call.

'They won't have her back,' she told Hazel, who returned to her room and repeated everything to me: 'They said it was your biological father who took you away, so you can go and live with him now. They will pack up all your things and send them to his house. And then that rude bastard slammed the phone down on Mum.'

I could hardly utter a word when Hazel told me that. My God, it meant I was actually homeless! Next, she asked for my father's number so her mum could call him.

'She can't come back here,' was his terse answer.

It was Hazel's mum who came into the room then: 'Have you got someone else you can call?'

'My aunt, I suppose,' I managed to say between more hiccupping sobs as I passed her my phone with Aunt Mary's number in it.

So down she went and made that call.

'She's coming over to collect you in about an hour or so,' she told me, before asking if I had eaten anything. When I shook my head, she went downstairs again and then a few minutes later, she brought me up a tray with some fruit juice and a sandwich, which I could hardly swallow.

'Of course you could have stayed here for a while, Ava, but it's better if someone from your family sorts this mess out. I don't want you to think you're not welcome here though because you absolutely are,' she told me.

At this, there were more tears – seems kindness has that effect on me.

About an hour later I heard the doorbell ring and I knew that my aunt had arrived. The two women must have talked for a while and then Aunt Mary came up to the room and put her arms around me: 'Let's get you back to my house and we can talk there,' she said gently.

She didn't ask many questions on that drive – clearly, she already knew about my parents refusing to have me back.

* * *

I stayed with Aunty Mary, Uncle Harry and my cousins in their house for several days until my aunt told me that my father had decided he would have me back and yes, he would arrange for me to go to a school near him.

'I think it's better for you to be away from this area for a while, so you can get over everything,' she added. In other words, she believed that given time, she could persuade her sister to make it up with me.

Being told that I was going back to Dad's house did not give me a warm, fuzzy feeling. I knew it was because he stood no choice. After all, he had taken me away from Mum and Ed and he had caused the problem. I wished I had never run away from Leicester. *Why had I got myself into this mess?* I kept asking myself. Because I thought my real dad loved me and I was welcome in their house.

That was my big mistake – and sadly, it was not to be the last one I would make.

36

Dad arrived on the Saturday morning. Of course my aunt, who I knew still couldn't stand the man, was polite enough to invite him in. I don't know what was said between them but after about twenty minutes, Aunt Mary came up to the little box room where I had been staying to tell me that everything was all right.

'You have my phone number,' she told me. 'Just ring me if you have any problems.'

'I will,' I said, even though I was more than a little disappointed that she had not arranged for me to live with her. The reason she had given me was that she felt that I would be better off away from the area. More than once she had told me that staying a good few miles away from my parents would be advisable but I just assumed it was because she did not wish to be involved in a family row. She looked after my little sister when Mum was at work, but while I was there Dawn had not been seen, which I suppose explains her and my uncle's decision.

'There's a good local school that your father has arranged for you to go to and I want you to work hard there; you need to catch up on all this lost time.' And her last words to me were: 'Work hard and pass those exams next year.' Giving me a hug, she slipped an envelope into my hand. 'A little pocket money for you, Ava,' she said with a kindly smile.

She had gone to her sister's and picked up my clothes, which were packed in a big case. My books were in a box but it seemed that my cassette player and music, the cause of so much trouble, were missing. When I came downstairs, Dad picked everything up and said nothing more to me other than 'Let's go, Ava.'

That drive was different from the first one. No stopping for a coffee, no Liza wanting to talk to me on the phone and very little conversation from Dad, though he did pass me a cigarette. I was completely aware that taking me back to his home was about the last thing he wanted to do but not a word was spoken about the circumstances of my return.

When we arrived, there was no sign of Liza, let alone her eagerly running out to greet me. Just a rather icy silence when Dad and I went into the kitchen. Liza simply said, 'Hello Ava,' but not in a very friendly way and her facial expression said it all. I wondered how on earth I was going to stick it out there if I was so unwanted.

My spirits lifted a little when Jonny appeared. Smiling away, he insisted on carrying my case upstairs for me. 'It's nice to have you back, sis,' he told me when we went into my room and I felt some of my anxiety leaving me because I believed he really meant it.

To begin with I saw Jonny as being a pretty together and kind young guy. He seemed to love the fact that he had reconnected with his younger sister, who had been kept from him for so long. And I liked the fact that I felt I had one really good friend in that unwelcoming house. It seemed that when he was around he did his best to protect me from Liza's temper. She certainly made no effort to hide how much she resented me being there. Liza targeted me at every chance she got to make me look small, whether it was something I had said, something I wore, or even something I was reading. I was too young to accept that she didn't like me or understand that the best way to handle her was to be polite and keep as much distance as possible. But I was a teenager who didn't have that sort of insight and maturity – after all, I had also felt unloved so many times when I lived with Mum and Ed.

I wanted to try and win Liza over. So much so that when she acted as though we were friendly, she manipulated the situation so she could get every bit of information out of me. There I was feeling grateful because my stepmother had actually smiled in my direction or included me in a conversation. So, what did I do? Told her my secrets – you know, typical teenage ones. Such as my parents' hateful attitudes to my friends and how my sister was loved more than me, just about everything that had bothered me for so many years. Then when she appeared to be sympathetic, I brought up Greg. How I had felt all weak at the knees when he smiled at me in class and how my body tingled when he kissed me – you know how teenagers are, we seek to confide that sort of thing. Well, that was pretty naive of me, wasn't it? I had just handed her verbal weapons she could use to embarrass me. And Liza, being Liza, did not waste any time doing that.

Jonny must have seen how her bitchy remarks were wearing me down. 'Come on, Ava, let's go out and stretch our legs a bit,' he would say with a friendly grin and I would jump up and follow him out of the house into the fields that it backed onto. Out would come a packet of cigarettes from Jonny's pocket and he would light one for me and one for him. I felt he was being kind because he was annoyed about how Liza was treating me.

* * *

There was one time when Liza was so horrible that I was reduced to floods of tears. At home I was never embarrassed if my underwear got some blood on it when my period came and I just put it in the washing basket. Which I thought was all right to do at Dad's house.

Clearly it wasn't.

Liza screamed at me, 'Ava, you nasty, filthy, fucking girl, come here immediately!'

I came running out of my room, not realising at first what was going on. My father ran up the stairs, my brother came out of his room to find Liz standing next to the linen basket on the landing, my blood-stained underwear in her hand. She began waving it around, shouting for everyone to look at how disgusting I was. I was so humiliated, I wanted the earth to open up and swallow me. No one else said a word or attempted to stop her, they all stood there staring at me until I ran back to my room.

That's just one example of how she wore me down until I was no longer the confident teenager I had once been. It was one of many other things she did to belittle me, but that was certainly one of the worst examples of her behaviour – the most embarrassing too. I mean, in front of Dad and Jonny.

Day after day, I felt more defeated. She was worse than both my parents put together. How I wished I had stayed with my mum and just waited things out until I was older and better equipped to deal with the dramas I had there. In Dad's house I simply wasn't able to cope with a woman like Liza and his indifference to her attitude and the insults she directed to me. Her pregnancy was by now very advanced and he went along to appointments with her every time.

It was the evening after that tawdry scene when Jonny, noticing I was still upset, introduced me to dope, or weed as he called it. When he rolled the first joint, lit it and inhaled pretty deeply himself, he then passed it to me: 'Now take a deep drag into your lungs and all your worries will float away, you'll see.' He was right – they did – and by the time the joint was finished, we found ourselves giggling away. But that didn't stop me feeling so alone when I woke up the next morning. I was desperate for someone to be on my side and there was only Jonny, who I believed was there for me.

Gradually over the next few weeks, I began to smoke much more dope – it seemed to make the world look like a more beautiful place. Though the cheap wine Jonny gave me as well helped turn me into a sickly drunk, who lurched all over the place. It was he then who helped get me into the house and up the stairs without being heard. I went into my room and crawled into bed, my head spinning. Good thing that everyone else was sound asleep, or so I hoped.

Dope might have made me feel better, but it hardly helped with my classes or my homework. My grades had dropped right down at the new school – I just couldn't find my old determination to try to do well. The only person I felt I could lean on was Jonny and at the time he was the one person I believed cared for me. I could see how Liza hated seeing us getting on so well. It made her even more bitchy, if that was possible. It was clear that as she had a daughter, she expected him to pay her attention and play the part of the older brother to her and not me, even if she was only five.

As I felt I was becoming closer to Jonny while we were sitting outside smoking more reefers, I heard more about how he felt over Mum leaving. He couldn't remember what it was like when he was with her and Dad, or how he ended living with his own father once he and Liza became an item. Liza had told him that Dad was very angry when Mum left, but Jonny was frustrated at not knowing for himself how everything had played out.

'Not that toddlers do remember much,' I pointed out while trying to see things from his point of view.

He opened a bottle of beer, took another drag on a reefer and told me what he believed was the truth of what happened to him. Or rather what Liza had over the years planted in his mind. She might have been an attractive woman with a certain charm, but I had already seen that Liza had no warmth or empathy for another woman's child. She was jealous of Mum, the woman my dad still hated for leaving him and jealous of me, his eldest daughter.

When Jonny told me about the stories that had come from

Liza, it was clear that she was determined to wipe out any good memories of Mum. In his mind, our mother had taken him and me when she left, only leaving Luke behind: 'She didn't really want me though,' he said.

I tried to tell him that this version of events wasn't true.

'She brought me back and dumped me with Dad and Liza, didn't she?' he insisted.

I could hardly work out what he was saying because this was nothing like what Luke, Mum and Ed had told me.

'And she kept you with her, so she couldn't have loved me, could she?'

Again, I tried to explain that I was too little not to be with my mother as she was still breastfeeding me but it had no effect on his warped perception of the circumstances of Mum leaving. Which was no wonder when I heard word for word the story Liza had told him: 'Your mother did not love you,' she had told him repeatedly. 'Let me tell you what she did. She left her husband for another man, taking you and Ava with her. And then, after he and I got together, she came to our house with you and dumped you. Walked in as though she belonged there, pulling you along with her – "He needs to be with his dad" was her excuse and I felt so sorry for you. You appeared to be completely bewildered so I let her walk into the kitchen.

'I told your mum that your dad wouldn't be back for about an hour. And do you know what she said then, Jonny? "I know that and no, I don't want to wait for him. It's Jonny who needs to see him, not me." With that, she picked me up and popped me on the kitchen table before Liza could ask her what she was doing.

'So, your mother just said to me, "Your dad will be here to see you soon, I don't want you anymore." Then she dumped the carrier bag she had brought with her. "His clothes," she said to Liza. She told me I was sobbing my little heart out and all your mum could do was turn around and walk out of the door.'

'But Luke must have told you that wasn't true,' I protested.

'He did, but I don't believe him. He doesn't get on with Dad so he started cosying up to your mother to annoy our father. So, he would lie to stick up for her. Anyhow, he hardly ever comes here now, thank goodness.'

I managed to stop myself from telling him what I had been told by Mum, Ed and Luke. That she had left both the boys when she ran off. Which didn't stop her wanting to see her sons. But when she went to the house she had left, the door was slammed in her face so hard, it nearly caught her fingers, which were resting on the door jamb. She wrote to him, phoned repeatedly and tried everything to get him to allow her to see them. Right up until my sister Dawn was born and then she gave up.

What truly saddened me was when he met her a few years earlier, couldn't he see how much she had missed him? If I could, why couldn't he? Because he didn't want to, I realised later, was the real answer to that question. I know Mum could be a bit of a bitch, but I didn't believe a word of what Jonny told me. However, Jonny did. I guess it was that which had caused the dark side of him, which I was soon to meet. Not that I was aware of it until then. To me, he was my only escape, while to him, getting me hooked on dope and alcohol was his leverage. My brother wanted me to feel dependent on him. He could drive and because we lived in a remote village that felt so far from anywhere, he was my only way of escaping from the house. He must have known I was desperate to flee those four walls where I had to put up with Liza's sniping and Dad's indifference. Also, he knew that the more miserable I got, the more I wanted to smoke dope and swallow alcohol. Two things that he was more than happy to provide, if it got me under his control.

There were evenings when, knowing that everyone was asleep, Jonny would open my bedroom door quietly and whisper for me to come with him or wave a spliff in the air to indicate that he was going for a smoke in the garage, where his car was kept. There we would sit, puffing away and chatting, until we were both stoned and then we'd creep back to our rooms. Once he was pretty sure that I couldn't do without the combination of alcohol and dope, he finally showed his true self. It was when we were sitting close to each other in his car that he grabbed my leg hard, leaned across me and kissed me: a wet, open-mouth kiss that made me want to scrub my face clean. I can't tell you why I didn't scream or stop him, it was almost as if I were paralysed. He grabbed my private parts … I felt sick. I felt … I can't even find the words …

I just let him.

So, why did I let him? I can't explain, it was like my best friend was gone. He wasn't that person I trusted, I thought he had my back, but from the expression on my brother's face, I knew why he had done this.

37

After that assault in the car, I was someone else. I felt like a
child, not the teenager I actually was. If I could go back in
time, I would tell my younger self to hold on to her courage, use arms, legs, feet and even teeth and nails to fight him
off, shout out he was sick and he'd better get his filthy hands
off me. But in reality, when you trust someone and become
so dependent on them, the shock of them showing their real
self is numbing. It almost made me feel like nothing was
really happening.

But it was.

And it continued.

Most evenings, he would suggest one of our usual walks
in front of Liza, making it impossible for me to say no. She
knew my homework was finished, though not how badly I
had done it.

More dope being smoked outside, more cheap wine being
swallowed, before his hands would begin creeping over to my
body. My breasts were the first place his hands aimed for, the

second my crotch. I would try wriggling away, only to hear him laugh: 'Get real, Ava! If you make an enemy of me, who have you got left for company? Face up to the fact that there's no one who wants you.' I might have hated him for taunting me like this, but I already knew that those cruel words were true. I was counting the months to my sixteenth birthday, not that it would make much difference to anyone in the house, for they hadn't noticed my fifteenth one. I had heard nothing from my parents either; not even a text or card arrived from them, let alone a present. My little sister, who had made me such a beautiful card the year before, also ignored it. Though I did have a few nice texts from friends, my brother Luke and my Aunt Mary.

Anyhow, I knew that the law stated that at sixteen, I could leave home. I'm sure that Liza did too; I bet she couldn't wait. Not that I had a clue how I was going to look after myself. I would have to get some sort of job and find somewhere to live, I supposed, but where? I kept telling myself that I'd work something out and anyhow, there were hostels, weren't there?

What I didn't know then was that Jonny was also counting the days off.

I did my best to make Jonny believe that it was really wrong for a brother to touch up his sister though not wanting to rile him anymore, I held back the fact that as I was under-age, it was also against the law. Not that he would have been bothered, just telling him it was wrong made him snigger away with something akin to delight.

I gradually began to realise that it was not just Mum that Jonny hated, it was me as well. Something that I found so very hard to accept but when I did, I understood his reason for masquerading as my friend. I worked out that it was so he could make me reliant on him which, by the time it dawned on me, I already was. I needed those spliffs to see the world as a better place and viewing it through stoned eyes and alcohol also helped me sleep. But I didn't need him mauling me. I just couldn't see what I could do to make him stop. Dad and Liza had seen us getting on so well, there was no way they would believe anything bad I said about him. Jonny knew that and so did I.

What I hadn't worked out was, thanks to the memories that Liza had planted in his head, Jonny had a plan mapped out to get his revenge. Revenge on the sister who had taken his place in his mother's affections. Had he remained the youngest, his twisted mind told him it would have been him she would have taken and not returned like unwanted goods.

One day he waited patiently until everyone, including our new baby boy and half-sister, was out shopping, to put the first part of his plan in place. We had been told to help ourselves to food as after their weekly shop, Dad, Liza and Eve were having lunch out with a couple of friends who wanted to see the new baby.

Jonny must have rubbed his hands with glee when he heard that they were going to be out for quite a long time. To him, that meant there would be just the two of us in the house for quite some time. Without neighbours nearby and the family out, it wouldn't have mattered one iota if I screamed my head off when, within minutes of them leaving, he pounced. Twisting my arm and forcing me down to my knees, he placed a foot on my back and pushed hard so I lay flat and then yanked off my jeans before flipping me over.

That was the first time he raped me, but not the last. However much I struggled, he was too strong for me. I kept begging him to stop, but he didn't and I suspect my pleas excited him more. It hadn't taken long in reality, but to me it felt like it lasted forever. I could hear his gloating words, 'Say goodbye to your virginity, Ava,' as he pushed into me as hard as he could. I felt a searing pain shoot through my body and knew what he had done. I cried then.

When I finally managed to get up, I was sore – my body hurt, my legs felt wobbly and I wanted to get the smell of his body off me. There were spots of blood on my thighs, making me feel completely defiled. Grabbing my clothes, I ran out of the sitting room and up the stairs to my bedroom. It was the shower I wanted first. I don't know how long I stayed under it; I washed away those small drops of blood, using a flannel to scrub between my legs over and over again until I felt raw. Backwards and forwards I swayed, holding on to the taps, as my knees kept dipping and it seemed that they were unable to hold me up straight. Finally, I switched the shower off and wrapping myself in a towel, crawled into my bed, where I stayed for the rest of the day.

Jonny always wore a certain brand of cologne and to this day when I recognise this smell on others in a shop or in the street, it places pictures of him forcing me time after time to give in, while whispering in my ear, 'No one's going to believe you, Ava, even if you try to tell them.'

There were so many nights and seized moments to follow

that were just like this. I was his victim, the one who was to blame for his mother abandoning him. That first time, when darkness came, I just remember staring at my bedroom wall, seeing the shadows cast by moonlight shining through the window and feeling the last of my innocent childhood disappear, tears dripping down my face. It was then that I thought of Mum. I know it might sound weird after everything that had happened, but I wanted her with me so badly.

Even now, I can't wipe out the memories of that year when I felt trapped in my father's house. The one that hardly ever leaves me is the last time Jonny came into my room: it was early in the morning on a Saturday and not having to go to school, I was still half asleep.

'Hey there, Ava,' he said and I shot up in bed, instantly wide awake and alert, knowing straight away why he was there. I could hear it in his voice and see in his eyes that his sole intent was to rape me again. When I tried to jump out of bed, he was too fast for me and with one shove I fell back onto the pillows, which gave him the opportunity to yank my pyjama bottoms down to my ankles. Just recounting this makes me feel both my younger self and my adult one too cringing at what I'm saying but I have to get out what actually happened because that was where things finally came to a head. Just as he began to rub himself against me and lower one hand to unzip his fly, Liza came barging in. The first reaction I felt was relief. She would stop him raping me, for I just could not bear the thought of him being inside me again. To my horror, the anger on her face was directed at me. My feeling of relief vanished to be replaced by dismay and fear:

Oh shit, this isn't happening to me, went through my head. As Jonny jumped off me, it gave me the opportunity to pull my pyjama bottoms up.

Liza did not say a word, nor did Jonny, which made me feel even more frightened. They just looked at each other and walked out. I heard their steps going down the stairs and a little later, there was the click of the front door opening and shutting. I could hardly believe it; they had left the house. Maybe they wanted to talk about what had happened without my half-sister hearing? It must have been about forty minutes later that I heard them returning but where they had gone to, I have no idea. I just sat in my room, thinking about what had just occurred. Where was the yelling? Where was the phone call to Dad, who must have gone into work or out to play golf? Liza should have been horrified at what he was doing. It's not as though Jonny was her son, surely she must be appalled at him raping his younger sister?

A little later when I crept to the top of the stairs, I could hear Liza was on the phone, but not what she was saying. I shot back to my room and got showered and dressed – I felt I had no other choice but to wait and see what was going to happen.

Minutes passed and then I heard her coming up to my room. She just looked coldly at me. When she came in, she addressed me quite formally: 'There's nothing I want to say or hear from you until your dad gets back here.' Then she set a tray of food down on my bedside table, told me to stay exactly where I was and left. That certainly told me whose side she was on. I didn't even try to say anything, I knew there was no point. For her to have rushed into my room like that, she must have known that something was happening. I had a horrible feeling that she had known all along. My brother's drinking and smoking weed could hardly have been a secret. You know, the whole time I lived there, I learnt that saying nothing was better than trying to defend myself. And this time I just knew that somehow it was me who was going to be seen as the villain, not Jonny. Apparently, as I was soon to find out, numbers don't lie. And by numbers, I mean them: there was Liza and Jonny and then me. My fingers were crossed that my father would take my side, for no matter what, it was statutory rape.

When I heard Dad come home, I waited to be called down, which I was after about an hour. As I walked into the room, both he and Jonny were standing fairly close together. *Not a good sign*, my inner voice said. My father looked at me and I could see he was utterly shocked at what he had just heard. I waited for him to at least ask me for my side of the story but no, nothing like that was going to happen. Dad just said to both Jonny and Liza that he was so sorry he had brought me into their home; that it was all his fault that I had seduced his son. So, there you go ... shocking, isn't it? Jonny's and my story had been set and cemented: I was the one who had made this happen apparently. I was, as Dad said, 'an incestuous little participant'.

After he had flung those stinging words out, my father sent me to my room. No one wanted to hear my lies, is what he told me. I can't tell you why I didn't scream that what they were saying was also abuse. For almost a year Jonny had taken advantage of me and I had hated every minute, every smell and every feeling that went through me. But I said nothing and went back to my bedroom. And you know what? I slept.

No knock at my door, no Jonny, not even supper – nothing but deadly silence.

*　*　*

The next day I had a weird moment with Liza: she asked if I wanted to come on a walk with her. After offering me a cigarette, she looked at me in a way she never had before – it was like she was sad for me. All she said then was, 'If this gets out, stick up for yourself, Ava. I know, even if your dad doesn't, what Jonny has done.' I still haven't worked out her reasoning for once we were back in the house again, she was her usual bitchy self.

I did my best to stay out of everyone's way.

But Jonny hadn't finished his act of revenge, which I realised when he came into my room for the last time. Not to rape me, but to pull me out of bed and threaten to beat me if I went to the police. Liza was behind him, just staring. They won. I broke and screamed the words they wanted to hear: 'I'm going!' I said – and I did, I just pulled a few things out of my cupboard, stuffed them in my rucksack, walked out of the house and kept walking till I reached the long road back to Loughborough.

I never looked back and I've never seen or contacted them since. Which doesn't stop me from seeing Jonny's face staring down at me from time to time in a nightmare. But that's a picture I quickly force to the back of my head as soon as I wake in a cold sweat.

* * *

That night, for the first time in my life I slept on a park bench. It's a wonder that I wasn't raped, killed or robbed over the next few days. I doubt if I looked worth messing with. Luckily, I still had that envelope Aunt Betty had given me. Inside it was fifty pounds. If only she had let me stay with her, I wouldn't have been homeless on the day I turned sixteen – the day both Liza and Jonny made sure I left. I wanted to ring her but then I just couldn't bring myself to face her – she would have been so shocked to hear what had happened.

So, what happened next? I met up with a few people I knew, was able to do some sofa surfing and even managed to get a part-time job at McDonald's for a little while. The worst memory I have of that time was not being mugged – which I was – but seeing my mother. I was on the tills one Saturday and looking up, I saw Mum standing in front of me. I just didn't know what to do, what to say. Nor, I think, did she. We just stood there, shocked. For some inexplicable reason, I rushed into the manager's empty office. I took a few deep breaths and came back, only to find that she had gone.

That was the last time I saw her. There are so many things I wish I had been able to say to her that day, so many things I want her to know – how her abandoned son raped me and how, despite everything, there were so many times when I had wanted to be with her. But that day she made it clear that she didn't need me in her life ever again.

She will never know how much that hurts.

It was then, knowing I would never see my family again, that I called Hazel. My old schoolfriend just asked where I was and told me she was coming over. She took me back home with her and comforted me when I told her everything that had happened since we said goodbye as I left with Dad. I stayed with her until she found me two things: a bedsit and a job.

And then what happened? We went out to celebrate my first pay-packet.

And then a good-looking man joined us.

Remember Dave?

Epilogue

Today, it's ten years since I left the refuge and a lot has happened since then. I'm not saying that those years were as good as I could possibly make them. I'm sure that some of you who have read my story will also have been in dark places and that you too have memories that you want to disappear from your mind so let me be honest here: it's never easy to erase the past, that takes time. But we have to tell ourselves more than once that to move on, we must fight to stop our past from ruining our future.

Maybe it was being determined to give my children a happy and secure background that gave me even more reason to put it all behind me. They needed a strong mother who could guide them through their early years so that one day they would be confident, independent people. Of course there were days when I felt down and it was one such day when my biggest worry – the one that had tormented me for over a year – disappeared. It didn't take place on one of those bright sunny days that lift our spirits when it happened either; it was a dull afternoon in the middle of the week, when with a grey sky over my head and puddles under my feet, I had gone to fetch my son from school. That day, like every weekday, I was at the school gates sheltering under my umbrella as those dark clouds had chosen to rain down on us just as the mothers and the occasional father gathered. Small wonder that I was not in the best of moods as I waited. It was only when I saw Justin, his little face creased into a wide smile, running towards me, that I too felt a matching one stretch across my face. Though it was not as wide as the next one when he said, 'Hi Mum.' I nearly burst into tears, I could hardly believe he was finally speaking.

The mother next to me patted my arm for she knew about his silence and we both smiled as his teacher came out of the school, beaming – 'There you are, Ava, we said he would speak when he was ready and it looks like he is.' I was still so choked up that all I could do was bend down and hug my boy, tears of joy streaming down my face.

A few minutes later when we were on the bus, he began telling me all about his day at school. In fact, he hardly paused to draw breath. God, I was happy! And isn't it those kind of things that make us feel everything we have struggled to do has been worthwhile?

Having one less worry made me even more determined to work hard for my children's future. It stopped me from walking out of the club I so detested – I needed enough money tucked away not to have to worry about the bills.

My life for the following year had to be well compartmentalised. I had days of attending classes and hours of study as well as collecting my children from the school and nursery. Good thing I was still only twenty-three – at least I had a good amount of much-needed energy. And in case you're wondering how did my two get to school and nursery, my good friend Jean took them there for almost the whole of that twelve months while I succeeded in gaining a diploma in health studies, as well as passing my A-levels in maths and science.

Was that enough then? I had passed the exams that I hadn't been able to take earlier because I hadn't stayed at school long enough. Those pieces of paper would help me find a decent job, wouldn't they? Not necessarily one that paid enough, I thought, after checking the salaries for the jobs I could have applied for. And that's when I had to decide: get some sort of job and enjoy some adult company, or put my life on hold a little longer and aim for a degree course. So, I chose the latter – I wanted to be a successful woman by the time my kids were at senior school. It wasn't just for them, I so needed it for my self-esteem as well.

I looked up universities offering online degree courses and filled in numerous application forms. Within a matter of weeks, I was enrolled for an undergraduate degree in the subjects I was more than interested in: psychology and criminal behaviour.

Why those subjects?

At least, I suspected, I already knew more about those subjects than a lot of eighteen-year-olds would when they went up to university. Nothing like turning a negative into a positive! It meant that some of my past could actually be useful to me – who would have thought it? So if yours could too, don't hesitate in using it to your advantage!

I left the club when I signed up for my degree course. There were online tutorials, projects and research to do when my two had been tucked into their beds. Yes, Jade was now in the bottom bunk and Justin loved being up top – how time had flown with those two growing up so fast. I might have hated the club life but thank goodness, I had been able to put enough away to make sure my children wouldn't go without. Because the three-year degree course I had signed up to was ambitious and once I began it, I wouldn't be able to work. I knew it would take up every minute of my spare time if I was going to get that degree. *It's for the future of the three of us*, I told myself. Though I did stop my studies when my son wanted me to help with a drawing or some arithmetic and I took great pleasure in listening to my daughter chattering away in her own baby language. And then head down, I continued my studies.

Those three years passed faster than I could have imagined. When I was awarded my degree, it seemed a lifetime away from when I first heard of Access and looked into doing my A-levels. Now you might have expected me to have looked for a good job, one where I could dress smartly and be able to pay for a childminder for Jade, someone who would also collect Justin from school for me. But no. Right from the beginning, I had decided it was not for me. The career path that I was waiting for my feet to walk down was teaching – I think I must have made up my mind the day I met Justin's teacher and the school Head.

The other positive was I would be able to spend more time with my children and even better, help them with their homework as they went through their education! A win-win situation all round, I reckoned. Because more than anything, I wanted to be the one who was there for them and be the person who could set them a good example.

My second ambition was to move away from the area. True, I had made some good friends there, especially Jean and Hils, who I knew I would miss. When I told them separately what I had decided to do, both of them wished me luck. 'You keep in touch,' they said. Which I promised to do, and I have. But my initial concerns about the drug dealers on the estate had not gone away. They were around and seemed to be getting even younger children under their control. Then just when I thought it was almost impossible to get a home in another area, I was burgled. Not the greatest experience, but at least one good thing came out of it: I was assisted by the council to move to a town where I felt my children would be safer.

I had applied for a teacher's training course and reading what would be expected of the students, any paid work during that time would be out of the question although it wasn't for the time between making the application and being accepted. Good thing I had a couple of skills that my previous life had given me: nothing like living with a man whose temper would explode if there was one tiny thing out of place. It meant I had become ace at cleaning. And hadn't my mother pushed me into going to those swimming lessons in the hope that I would make more white friends? She and Ed seemed to believe that swimming was a white children's sport. It might not have worked for Mum, but it did for me. I loved swimming and I still have the list of races I won in regional competitions so there was no need to worry about what I could do to earn money. I could clean offices in the early mornings until they shone and do the same at night when the staff, leaving wastepaper baskets full of empty takeaway containers, had taken themselves off home or to the nearest pub. That was one job I was given straight away without hesitation. The second one I applied for was to work at the local gym as a swimming instructor and that I got as well, especially when I presented them with my list of gala successes.

I made some good friends at the swimming club, one of them being Steve. He told me he had a girlfriend and we became good work friends. He was going through rather a bad time, not that he talked about it – his stepmum had cancer and his dad was also ill with COPD, so breathing was really difficult for him. Over the next twelve months we built up a warm friendship and then Covid appeared, causing the gym to abruptly close and all of us stayed in our homes. It was quite a long time before we met up again. The pandemic had been bad for him for both his stepmum and father had died and as we all know, during that time no one could sit by the hospital bed of someone they loved to help them in their final hours. He had also split up from his partner during the challenging months of lockdown.

Our friendship continued and yes, as you have most probably already guessed, it gradually grew deeper. I suppose this is the part where I should say what he looks like. He's taller than me and I'm 5'8", he has dark hair and a small beard. But it's not what he looks like that made me fall for him, it's who he is – warm, caring, generous and supportive.

I was still nervous about relationships when I suddenly realised that I was actually in one and not just a little scared that I might have made another mistake, but also worried about how my children would accept another person in my life. To cut a long story short, both my thirteen-year-old son and my feisty eight-year-old daughter liked him the moment they met him. They loved his cooking as well as him, for he was the one, who after a day's work, told me to get on with studying while he made the evening meal. He is the one who has shown not just me, but my children as well, what makes a relationship a really good one. The four of us celebrated Christmas 2021 together and I felt then that we were becoming a real family, where there was caring, love and laughter.

A few days later, at a minute before midnight, we opened some bubbles to welcome the new year in. It was after the bells had rung out, telling us that the old year had been usurped, I was to find out, by an even better one than the year before. Just after midnight, Steve proposed – and I accepted joyfully. The kids were thrilled too.

A few weeks later, I received my teacher's degree. Now I could look for the work I really wanted to do. And during the last week in April, a letter came through the door to tell me I had secured the job teaching at the senior school I had applied to.

I feel such pride in my children and in myself as well.

It might have taken ten years for me to get there, but to me, every moment was worth it.

So why did I want my story out there? To say to others that you must never let your hardships define you. We need to keep telling ourselves what it is we want from life and then fight for it every single day.

Was I nervous about my story being written?

Yes, although I knew who it was I wanted to contact: a bestselling writer whose autobiography I had just read. So, taking a deep breath, I pressed 'send' on my message on Messenger that I had just written to her ...

Acknowledgements

Today, I would like to take this opportunity to thank those whom in my darkest moments reminded me of the good in people.

Firstly, to my beautiful son and daughter, you gave me the strength to fight and strive to be the best woman and mother I could possibly be. I cannot put into words just how proud of you I am. Above all else, I love and thank you both. To my partner and best friend, because of you, I am finally complete. Since meeting you, I have laughter, love and safety. You make me so happy, I am so lucky to have you.

My aunt, you are one of the kindest people I know and continue to be someone I admire and respect to this day.

My eldest brother, you were there through some of my most difficult moments. The bond between our children shows how we have broken the cycle that our 'family' set out for us. Your amazing partner has become one of my true lifelong friends, and for that I am grateful.

To one of my oldest friends, I will never forget how you helped me.

Toni, because of you, I have peace. I can look forward in life and not dwell on the past. You are a true voice for those who have lost their own. I will forever be thankful for what you have done for me.

Ava Thomas

Refuge

www.nationaldahelpline.org.uk

The freephone, 24-hour national domestic abuse helpline:
0808 2000 247.

You can reach the Refuge helpline team using their secure
web form, or arrange a safe time for them to contact you.
Their team can also chat to you live online, Monday to
Friday, 3pm to 10pm.

Women's Aid

www.womensaid.org.uk

Women's Aid offer support via a live chat service, and you
can also email them at helpline@womensaid.org.uk.

They also run the Survivors' Forum, an anonymous space for
women over 18 who have been affected by domestic abuse,
where they can share their experiences and support one
another.

You can also contact refuge organisations through the police,
the Samaritans on 08457 90 90 90 (UK) or 1850 60 90 90
(ROI), social services or the Citizens Advice Bureau.

Available Now From

NO.1 BESTSELLING AUTHOR

TONI MAGUIRE

You can find more about Toni and her books at:

www.tonimaguire.co.uk

www.facebook.com/toni.maguire.page